GEORGIA'S CONFEDERATE MONUMENTS

GEORGIA'S
CONFEDERATE
MONUMENTS

IN HONOR OF A FALLEN NATION

GOULD B. HAGLER, JR.

MERCER UNIVERSITY PRESS | MACON, GEORGIA

For Gary Lane with
My best wishes.

Harold Holzer
5/10/16

MERCER
UNIVERSITY PRESS

Endowed by
TOM WATSON BROWN
and
THE WATSON-BROWN FOUNDATION, INC.

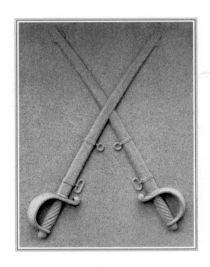

DEDICATED TO THE MEMORY
OF
THOMAS G. BARRETT
AND
STEPHEN D. COWEN

MUP/ H877
© 2014 Mercer University Press

Published by
Mercer University Press
1400 Coleman Avenue
Macon, Georgia 31207

First Edition
Books published by Mercer University Press are printed on acid-free paper
that meets the requirements of the American National Standard for Information Sciences—
Permanence of Paper for Printed Library Materials.

Book design by Burt&Burt

Library of Congress Cataloging-in-Publication Data

Hagler, Gould B., 1950-
Georgia's Confederate monuments: in honor of a fallen nation
Gould B. Hagler, Jr.
416 pages
Includes bibliographical references and index.
ISBN 978-0-88146-466-5 (hardback: alk. paper)
ISBN 0-88146-466-X (hardback: alk. paper)
1. Georgia—History—Civil War, 1861-1865—Monuments.
2. United States—History—Civil War, 1861-1865—Monuments.
3. Soldiers' monuments—Georgia.
4. War memorials--Georgia. I. Title.
E559.4.H34 2013
973.7'458—dc23
2013030162

Printed in the United States of America
9 8 7 6 5 4 3 2 1

ACKNOWLEDGMENTS

I wish to thank the persons listed below, and many others not named, whose generous financial support to Mercer University Press made the publication of this book possible.

CECIL D. DORSEY | GOULD B. HAGLER

MR. AND MRS. MICHAEL B. HAGLER | TOBIN B. HAGLER

WILLIAM AND GREER HAGLER | L. JACK SWERTFEGER, JR.

JAMES W. BOYD, JR. | FCCI INSURANCE GROUP

RICHARD AND CONNIE HAGLER | THE STEVE AND ALICE HAGLER FAMILY

ALICE HAGLER LEE | RANDALL PETERS

SUSAN SCHAFER AND BOB CAMERON | JACKSON H. SHERRILL, JR.

REPRESENTATIVE RICHARD H. SMITH

Many other people offered assistance of every kind and description. Warren Thomas, a descendant of one of the founders of the McNeel Marble Company, provided documentation on the monuments built by that company. Steve Davis gave me valuable advice in more ways than I can name. Benita Dodd assisted in reviewing the text for spelling, grammar and stylistic consistency.

More people than I can list responded to emails and phone calls to provide information about dates, builders, and the cost of specific monuments.

During the past two decades, I have spoken on the subject of Confederate monuments to Sons of Confederate Veterans camps, United Daughters of the Confederacy chapters, historical societies, Civil War Round Tables, and civic clubs. I learned a great deal from these audiences, and without exception I left the meetings armed with more information about Georgia's monuments and the people who made them. Thanks to all who attended and shared their knowledge with me — GBH.

. . .

With the exception of the picture taken at the 1910 unveiling of the Jasper County monument, all of the photographs in this book were taken by the author, most between 2009 and 2012. The subjects of four of the photographs are located on private property. The author wishes to thank the following for allowing access to their property and granting permission to publish the photographs: Oconee Hill Cemetery, Athens; the Georgia Trust for Historic Preservation, Atlanta; The Westview Cemetery, Inc., Atlanta; Fred D. Bentley, Sr., Kennesaw.

INTRODUCTION

In the decades following the Civil War, the people of Georgia built scores upon scores of monuments to honor the state's sons who fought and died for the Confederacy. The monuments began to go up within months of the Confederacy's fall.

The earliest monuments were an outgrowth of the work of local ladies' memorial associations, those sturdy women who organized the grisly work of taking the dead from hastily dug graves on or near battlefields and gave the fallen soldiers a proper burial. With the cemeteries laid out, with the Confederates' remains reinterred in marked graves, these ladies naturally erected monuments to pay homage to the memory of the dead.

The earlier monuments tend to be simple obelisks or other structures erected among Confederate graves. As time passed, the character and location of the monuments changed. The next phase of monument-building populated Georgia with statues of Confederate soldiers on city streets and courthouse squares. These monuments were most often the work of local chapters of the United Daughters of the Confederacy. Georgians passed by these monuments daily. They were reminded of the dead relatives they continued to mourn; however, as the conflict receded into the past the memorials took on two other purposes: to remind posterity of the Confederate soldiers' noble qualities and to state, often in very emphatic terms, the principles for which they fought. "Our Confederate Dead" was still inscribed on the front, but the other surfaces of the monument told their story of honor, duty, and bravery in defense of their principles.

The great era of monument-building was the waning years of the nineteenth century and the first fifteen years or so of the twentieth. While there was some variety, a regular pattern had taken shape: a soldier, armed and fitted out, stood on a column and oversaw the town and its people. The funereal motifs had yielded to martial symbols. The Daughters were honoring their aging fathers and their fallen comrades and telling their children what kind of men their forebears were.

By the 1920s the work seemed complete. It wasn't. Decades later, starting in the 1990s, a new round of building commenced. More than a dozen Confederate monuments—most the work of the Sons of Confederate Veterans—have been added to the inventory, and more are planned.

Most of the obelisks and statues honor the Confederates of the county in which they are placed. There are also monuments honoring specific men and the members of specific military units. There are several monuments dedicated to the women of the Confederacy. And, as one travels the state one also sees the odd boulder, fountain, stone slab, and arch—plus one Sigma Chi cross, one martyred lion, and one very tall chimney—all paying tribute to the people of the Confederate nation.

I have taken pains to get the best images possible of the monuments and their surroundings so the reader can appreciate these works of public art. The inscriptions on the monuments are also worthy of careful study. They relate an important story. They tell how the builders viewed their history. They state the South's reasons for seeking independence. They explain why the people of Georgia and other Southern states were willing to pay such a high price in this failed quest. They tell us how the people coped with the destruction of their beloved and short-lived Confederacy. They remind us that defeat is not dishonor.

Gould B. Hagler, Jr.
Dunwoody, Georgia
July 1, 2012

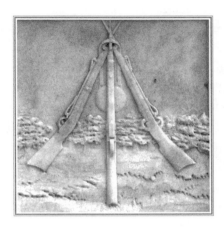

EXPLANATORY NOTES

DATES

Many of the monuments contain inscriptions indicating the date the monument was erected. If no other information is available, the text gives these dates. In some cases, the actual dates differ from the inscriptions. In these cases, the actual dates are given and the source of the information is cited. For monuments with no date inscribed, the dates are given when available and sources cited.

BUILDERS

Almost all Confederate monuments have inscriptions crediting the builders for their work, usually the ladies' memorial associations for the earlier monuments and the United Daughters of the Confederacy for those built after 1900 or so. Very few monuments credit the fabricators or artists. The McNeel Marble Company was the most active manufacturer of Georgia monuments during the heyday of construction. The fabricators (and artists for the unique sculptures) are named when the information is available.

"Builder" refers to the organization or organizations (or in rare cases, an individual) commissioning the monument. "Fabricator" refers to the company performing the work.

INSCRIPTIONS

The inscriptions are quoted so as to reproduce as faithfully as possible the format used on the monuments regarding capitalization, spacing, punctuation, and line breaks. Quotation marks are used only if they are present on the monuments. Every effort has been made to reproduce the inscriptions exactly as they appear.

The inscriptions frequently contain eccentric or clearly incorrect punctuation. Less often there are errors in spelling. Misspelled words are corrected without explanation, as are punctuation errors significant enough to be distracting. Inscriptions occasionally misquote poems or alter them slightly in ways that are intentional. The text quotes these poems as they appear and provides explanations where appropriate. Very few inscriptions name the author or the work quoted. The text provides this information where possible.

SOURCES

The sources most frequently cited are the works of McKenney, Wiggins, Widener, and UDC 2002. The citations for these sources contain no page numbers. Anyone wishing to consult these books can easily locate the information, as the monuments in these works are in alphabetical order by county (McKenney) or city (Wiggins, Widener, and UDC 2002).

Citations of other publications contain page numbers.

FLAGS

Monuments often contain carvings of Confederate flags. The text identifies the design of flags when the design is clear.

"Confederate Battle Flag" in the text refers to any square or rectangular flag covered entirely by the St. Andrew's cross. There were many other regimental battle flags, of course, but the design with the cross is the best known. No Georgia monument displays any other regimental flag.

Some monuments contain the First National, Second National, or Third National, and they are so identified in the text.

On some of the monuments, the flags' ratios seem incorrect, with the length too great in proportion to the width. The author consulted a vexillologist who advised that eccentric proportions were common with actual flags as well as with flags carved on monuments. The monuments' flags are identified without regard to their occasional odd shapes.

THE SOLDIERS' POSITIONS

The soldiers are most frequently described as standing "at rest." Close examination reveals subtle differences in the postures. No distinction is made between "in place rest" and "parade rest." Many of the statues are not in any stance that would be correct according to the manuals. One suspects that the flesh-and-blood soldiers tended to lack uniformity as do their marble likenesses. They were not professional soldiers, nor were most of their officers. They were citizen-soldiers, fighting for their country's survival. They were not overly concerned about how they looked on the parade ground.

Positions other than "at rest" are described as accurately as possible, but these also lack strict compliance with the manuals.

MATERIALS

For most entries, the text does not specify the materials from which the stone monuments are made. Usually the statues are made of marble and their supporting columns granite. Variations from this normal pattern are noted where appropriate.

THE SCOPE OF THIS BOOK

How many Confederate monuments are there in Georgia? This simple question has no simple answer.

There are approximately 140 statues, obelisks and other structures—built by local ladies' memorial associations, UDC chapters and other organizations—to honor the Confederate dead of their communities or those who lie buried in a Confederate cemetery. For these kinds of memorials, this book is intended to be comprehensive.

There are statues and other memorials to honor prominent individuals, such as generals John B. Gordon and James Longstreet. Other memorials honor units. The Irish Jasper Greens statue and the simple marker dedicated to the Middle River Volunteers are examples of this type. A few monuments pay tribute to the women of the Confederacy, the statues in Rome and Macon being the most elaborate. This book is intended to include all these as well.

After these we have a seemingly inexhaustible supply of other memorials related to the Confederacy and its people. Some monuments mark the location of specific events, such as reunions in Campbellton and Union Point. There are monuments to less prominent Confederates, such as the statue of Captain Matthew Nunnally. A stone marks the place where President Jefferson Davis spent his last night of freedom. Atlanta's Rhodes Hall contains beautiful stained-glass windows depicting scenes from Confederate history. Women who operated wayside homes for Confederate soldiers are honored in several communities. For memorials of this nature this book cannot be comprehensive, but some are included, as these also tell an important part of the story.

Several of the newer monuments honor the dead (or all veterans) of all American wars. These are included when they contain specific elements dedicated to the Confederacy.

The book does not include monuments in battlefield parks or graves of generals.

CSA   Confederate States of America (the obvious), Confederate States Army (also obvious), or Confederate Survivors' Association

LMA   Ladies' Memorial Association

SCS   Soil Conservation Service

SCV   Sons of Confederate Veterans

UCV   United Confederate Veterans

UDC   United Daughters of the Confederacy

USWV   United Spanish War Veterans

WPA   Works Progress Administration

GEORGIA CITIES AND COUNTIES

The monuments are listed by county. To assist the reader in locating monuments of interest, the lists starting on page 387 cross-reference the cities and counties in which the monuments are located. Campbell County, which contained three monuments, was abolished in 1932 and merged into Fulton County. These monuments are listed under Fulton County.

GEORGIA'S CONFEDERATE MONUMENTS

Appling County, Baxley

LOCATION: Courthouse grounds, facing West Parker Street	
DATE: 2008 (brochure from dedication ceremony)	
STYLE: Two bronze statues, a Confederate soldier and his wife	**BUILDER:** SCV

DEDICATED TO
THOSE WHO SACRIFICED ALL
SAVE HONOR.

CONFEDERATE STATES OF
AMERICA

1861–1865

ERECTED BY
APPLING GRAYS CAMP 918 SCV

COMPANY I, 27TH GEORGIA
VOLUNTEER INFANTRY
APPLING GRAYS

COMPANY F, 47TH GEORGIA
VOLUNTEER INFANTRY
APPLING RANGERS

CAPTAIN JOHN MAYERS' APPLING
COUNTY CAVALRY

CAPTAIN BEN MILIKIN'S APPLING
COUNTY MILITIA
COMPANY F, 1ST SYMON'S
RESERVES

COMPANY B, 54TH GEORGIA
VOLUNTEER INFANTRY APPLING
VOLUNTEERS

COMPANY K, 54TH GEORGIA
VOLUNTEER INFANTRY
SATILLA RIFLES

CO. A, CO. I AND CO. K CLINCH'S
4TH GEORGIA CAVALRY

CAPTAIN SILAS CROSBY'S APPLING
COUNTY MILITIA

The inscription appears on the pedestal beneath the statues. On each side is a marble headstone set on a fieldstone base. Inscriptions on the headstones name the companies in which local men served.

The soldier is holding his rifle, in a position similar to bayonet guard.

DEDICATED TO
THOSE WHO SACRIFICED ALL
SAVE HONOR

GEORGIA'S CONFEDERATE MONUMENTS

Atkinson County, Pearson

LOCATION: Courthouse grounds, Main Street	**DATE:** Ca. 2006 (Julian Haskins)
STYLE: Memorial stone	**BUILDER:** Julian Haskins

CARVED OUT OF THE
ENDURANCE OF
GRANITE,
GOD CREATED HIS
MASTERPIECE

THE
CONFEDERATE
SOLDIER
1861–1865
"DEO VINDICE"

Julian Haskins is a member of Sidney Lanier Camp 1908 of the SCV. He lives in Pearson. The monument cost approximately $3,000. Haskins paid for the monument with his own funds (conversation with Haskins, May 2012).

The quote on the monument is from Lillian Henderson, author of Roster of the Confederate Soldiers of Georgia, 1861–1865. This monument is one of three using this quote. The others are in Peach County and Whitfield County (the memorial wall in the Confederate Cemetery).

Baldwin County, Milledgeville

LOCATION: North Jefferson Street, opposite the entrance to Georgia Military College		
DATE: 1912	**STYLE:** Obelisk with two statues at the base	
BUILDER: UDC	**FABRICATOR:** McNeel Marble Co. (McNeel Memorials)	

THIS TRIBUTE TO THE
MEMORY OF THE
CONFEDERATE SOLDIER,
UNVEILED APRIL 26, 1912.

HIS HEROISM, IN THE
PRESENCE OF THE
CONQUERING FOE, WAS
EQUALLED ONLY BY
HIS GENEROSITY TO HIS
FALLEN ENEMY.

TO THE MEMORY OF THE
CONFEDERATE SOLDIER;
WHOSE FAME IS AS IMPERISH-
ABLE AS THE EVERLASTING HILLS;
WHOSE COURAGE IS UNRIVALLED
SINCE THE DAWN OF CIVILIZA-
TION; WHOSE NAME SHINES IN
UNDYING GLORY IN THE PAGES
OF HISTORY;

THIS MONUMENT IS LOVINGLY
ERECTED BY THE
ROBT. E. LEE CHAPTER
DAUGHTERS OF THE CONFEDERACY,
OF MILLEDGEVILLE GEORGIA.
HIS UNCONQUERABLE
PATRIOTISM AND SELF-
SACRIFICE RENDERED
ABORTIVE THE EFFORT
OF HIS ENEMIES,
AFTER HIS FLAG HAD
FOLDED FOREVER, TO
DESTROY HIS PROUD
INHERITANCE.

The dates of the war are carved on one surface. A CSA monogram appears opposite the dates. Bronze lion heads were the spouts for the now-inoperable fountains. A flag decorates one surface of the obelisk. The cavalryman is in the order arms position facing west; the infantryman is at rest facing east.

The monument's original location was the street between the courthouse and the post office. Endangered by traffic, it was moved to its present location in 1948. The 20-foot shaft is granite; the base and the statues are marble. The cost of the monument was $2,700 (McKenney).

GEORGIA'S CONFEDERATE MONUMENTS

Baldwin County, Milledgeville

LOCATION: Memory Hill Cemetery	**DATE**: 1868 (McKenney)
STYLE: Obelisk	**BUILDER**: LMA

OUR UNKNOWN
CONFEDERATE DEAD.

A marble tablet with the date 1868 was installed years after the dedication but is now gone; the cost was $300; this monument was the first in the state built "to honor generally the fallen soldiers" (McKenney).

The gravestones now contain the names of the fallen Confederates. There are two large stone urns at the base of the obelisk.

A bronze tablet, installed in 2003, lists the names and units of the once-unknown soldiers, all of whom served in the Georgia Militia. According to the tablet, they died in Brown Hospital in Milledgeville and Stout Hospital in Midway. Their identities were discovered in 2003.

Baldwin County, Milledgeville

LOCATION: Memory Hill Cemetery	**STYLE**: Obelisk	**BUILDER**: Governor Joseph E. Brown

IN MEMORY OF
COL. JOHN M. BROWN
BORN APRIL 12. 1839.
DIED
JULY 26. 1864.

THIS MONUMENT IS ERECTED
BY HIS BROTHER
JOSEPH E. BROWN.
IN COMMEMORATION OF HIS VIR-
TUES AS A GENTLEMAN A SOLDIER
AND A CHRISTIAN.

COL. BROWN
FELL WOUNDED IN THE
BATTLE BEFORE ATLANTA 22. JULY
1864. WHILE GALLANTLY LEADING HIS
REGIMENT IN A CHARGE ON A BATTERY
OF FEDERAL ARTILLERY. HE WAS A WARM
HEARTED SOUTHERN MAN AND WON HIS
RANK EARLY BY HIS REPEATED ACTS OF
HEROISM AND HIS CHIVALROUS BEAR-
ING IN DEFENCE OF HIS NATIVE STATE.
WHEREVER HE MET THE INVADING FOR-
CES WHO WERE REGARDED HER ENEMIES
HE NEVER FAILED TO STRIKE IN HER
DEFENCE.

The grave marker at the base reads:
C.S.A.
JNO. M. BROWN.
LIEUT. COL 2ND REGT
STATE TROOPS.

John M. Brown was the brother of Gov. Joseph E. Brown. Col. Brown was mortally wounded in the Battle of Atlanta on July 22, 1864 (Bragg, p. 89).

Banks County, Baldwin

LOCATION: South of Baldwin by 6 miles, at Georgia Highway 105 and Carnes Circle		

DATE: 1980	**STYLE**: Memorial stone	**BUILDERS**: Descendants of the soldiers

THIS MARKER IS A MEMORIAL
TO THE MIDDLE RIVER
VOLUNTEERS, MARCH 4, 1862,
WHO DRILLED ON THIS ROAD
FOR SERVICE BEFORE
ENTERING CIVIL WAR.
DONATED BY DESCENDANTS
OF THESE SOLDIERS.

DEDICATED 1980

There are crossed United States flags on the top of the monument's front face. Following the dedication is a company roster of 127 names, with officers and noncommissioned officers on the front, and privates on the rear. Those who died in the service are marked with crosses. Two of the five officers named and three of the seventeen noncommissioned officers died in the war. Forty-nine of the 105 privates lost their lives. Many of the soldiers were relatives. Among the privates, the dead include three of five men named Cash; two of three Caudells; two of the three Murrays; both Davises; both Wards; and both Segarses.

Baldwin lies partly in Habersham County and partly in Banks County. It is the town nearest the monument. It is peculiar that the only flags depicted are flags of the United States, not the Confederacy.

Bartow County, Cartersville

LOCATION: Old courthouse grounds, North Erwin Street	DATE: 1908 (McKenney)
STYLE: Statue of a solder on a column	BUILDER: UDC
FABRICATOR: McNeel Marble Co. (McNeel Memorials)	

OUR SOLDIERS

CONFEDERATE
STATES OF
AMERICA

LET THE STRANGER WHO MAY IN
FUTURE TIME READ THIS INSCRIPTION,
AND RECOGNIZE THAT THERE WERE
MEN,
WHOM POWER COULD NOT CORRUPT,
DEATH COULD NOT TERRIFY,
DEFEAT COULD NOT DISHONOR;
LET THESE VIRTUES PLEAD FOR
JUST JUDGEMENT IN THE CAUSE
—FOR WHICH THEY PERISHED.—
LET GEORGIA, REMEMBER THAT THE
STATE TAUGHT THEM HOW TO LIVE
AND HOW TO DIE; AND THAT FROM HER
BROKEN FORTUNES, SHE HAS
PRESERVED

FOR HER CHILDREN, THE PRICELESS
TREASURE OF HER MEMORIES,
TEACHING
ALL WHO MAY CLAIM THE SAME
BIRTH-RIGHT, THAT TRUTH, VIRTUE
AND PATRIOTISM ENDURE FOREVER.

ERECTED BY
THE DAUGHTERS OF
THE CONFEDERACY.
IN HONOR OF THE MEN,
OF BARTOW COUNTY,
WHO SERVED IN THE ARMY
OF THE CONFEDERATE
STATES OF AMERICA.
THOSE WHO FOUGHT AND LIVED,
AND THOSE WHO FOUGHT AND DIED.

MAY THIS SHAFT EVER CALL TO
MEMORY, THE STORY OF THE GLORY
OF THE MEN WHO WORE THE GRAY.

The front surface of the plinth contains a Confederate Battle Flag, partly furled on its staff. On the rear are crossed rifles. Pediments above the plinth have the dates of the war (front and rear) and "CSA" (on the sides).

The soldier is standing at rest, and the monument's cost was $2,000 (McKenney).

Variations of the first quote are common inscriptions on Confederate monuments. The passage was written by William Henry Trescot for the Confederate monument at the state house in Columbia, South Carolina, with reference, of course, to that state and its soldiers (Snowden, 2:820).

GEORGIA'S CONFEDERATE MONUMENTS

Bartow County, Cassville

LOCATION: Cassville Cemetery	DATE: 1878	STYLE: Obelisk	BUILDER: LMA

All four sides contain inscriptions inside recessed shields of marble.

DEDICATED TO THE
MEMORY OF
OUR SOUTHERN HEROES
BY THE LADIES
MEMORIAL ASSOCIATION
OF CASSVILLE.
A.D. 1878.

IS IT DEATH TO FALL FOR
FREEDOM'S CAUSE:

REST IN PEACE OUR OWN
SOUTHERN BRAVES.
YOU LOVED LIBERTY MORE
THAN LIFE.

IT IS BETTER TO HAVE FOUGHT
AND LOST, THAN NOT TO HAVE
FOUGHT AT ALL.

The Ladies' Memorial Association of Cassville began raising money in 1867 but was unsuccessful. The legislature appropriated $300 in 1872. The total cost was $550. The monument bears the date 1878; the marble tablets probably were added later (McKenney).

Bartow County, Cassville

LOCATION: Cassville Cemetery, down the hill from the large obelisk

DATE: 1889	STYLE: Small stone column	BUILDER: UDC

CONFEDERATE STATES
OF AMERICA
1861–1865

THESE HEAD-
STONES WERE
PLACED HERE MAY
1889. BY CASS-
VILLE CHAPTER,
GEORGIA DIVISION
UNITED DAUGH-
TERS OF THE
CONFEDERACY.
IN HONOR OF THOSE
WHO FELL WHILE
DEFENDING THE
RIGHTS OF THE
SOUTH. LONG MAY
THEIR MEMORY
LIVE.

OUR CONFEDERATE DEAD

SO LONG AS BREA-
THES A SOUTHERN
WOMAN; SO LONG
AS TIME SHALL
LAST; SO LONG
WILL SOUTHERN
WOMEN CHERISH
AND HONOR THE
MEMORY OF THE
CONFEDERATE
SOLDIER, AND MEET
ANNUALLY TO
STREW THEIR
RESTING PLACE
WITH CHOICEST
GARLANDS.

REST

Bartow County, Kingston

LOCATION: Kingston Cemetery	DATE: 1874	STYLE: Obelisk	BUILDER: LMA

ERECTED
BY
LADIES MEMORIAL
ASSOCIATION
1874
IN MEMORY OF THE
250
CONFEDERATE SOLDIERS
BURIED HERE.

The following appears on a separate tablet:
REPAIRED IN 1937 BY SCS CAMP GA 13,
CARTERSVILLE, GA. IN CO-OPERATION WITH
CONGRESSMAN M.C. TARVER, BARTOW, CO.
AND KINGSTON CITIZENS.

Bartow County, Kingston

| LOCATION: Kingston Cemetery | STYLE: Memorial stone |

KINGSTON MEMORIAL
TO OUR
CONFEDERATE VETERANS

A battle flag is engraved beside the inscription. In front of the gravestone are bricks showing the names of Kingston's Confederate veterans, their units, and their dates of birth and death.

TO THE FOUNDERS OF
WAYSIDE HOSPITAL

THIS IS A MEMORIAL TO THE
HUMANITARIAN FOUNDERS OF THE
KINGSTON WAYSIDE HOME WHICH WAS
THE FIRST CONFEDERATE HOSPITAL
TO THE PHYSICIANS AND CITIZENS
WHO SO KINDLY SUPPORTED IT, AND
TO THE 250 BRAVE CONFEDERATE
SOLDIERS WHO LIE BURIED HERE

DEPARTMENT
OF NATURAL
RESOURCES

DIVISION OF
STATE PARKS
HISTORIC SITES
& MONUMENTS

Bartow County, Kingston

LOCATION: Kingston Cemetery	**DATE**: 1951 (scrapbook kept at the Kingston Museum)
STYLE: Memorial stone	**BUILDER**: State of Georgia

TO THE FOUNDERS OF
WAYSIDE HOSPITAL

THIS IS A MEMORIAL TO THE
HUMANITARIAN FOUNDERS OF THE
KINGSTON WAYSIDE HOME, WHICH WAS
THE FIRST CONFEDERATE HOSPITAL;
TO THE PHYSICIANS AND CITIZENS
WHO SO KINDLY SUPPORTED IT; AND
TO THE 250 BRAVE CONFEDERATE
SOLDIERS WHO LIE BURIED HERE.

DEPARTMENT
OF NATURAL
RESOURCES

DIVISION OF
STATE PARKS
HISTORIC SITES
& MONUMENTS.

The Georgia state seal is engraved at the bottom of the slab.

See the entry for Union Point (Greene County) for a brief discussion of wayside homes.

ORIGINAL HOSPITAL SITE
OF WAYSIDE HOME

THIS IS THE SITE OF KINGSTON
WAYSIDE HOME, THE FIRST
CONFEDERATE HOSPITAL, ESTABLISHED
IN AUGUST, 1861 BY THE SOLDIERS
AID SOCIETY AND OTHER CITIZENS
OF THIS VICINITY. MORE THAN
40,000 SICK AND WOUNDED
CONFEDERATE SOLDIERS RECEIVED
NECESSARY MEDICAL ATTENTION
WITHIN ITS WALLS DURING THE THREE
YEARS IT WAS OPERATED.

DEPARTMENT
OF NATURAL
RESOURCES

DIVISION OF
STATE PARKS
HISTORIC SITES
& MONUMENTS

Bartow County, Kingston

LOCATION: Kingston Cemetery	**DATE:** 1951 (scrapbook kept at the Kingston Museum)
STYLE: Memorial stone	**BUILDER:** State of Georgia

ORIGINAL HOSPITAL SITE
OF WAYSIDE HOME

THIS IS THE SITE OF KINGSTON
WAYSIDE HOME, THE FIRST
CONFEDERATE HOSPITAL, ESTABLISHED
IN AUGUST, 1861, BY THE SOLDIERS
AID SOCIETY AND OTHER CITIZENS
OF THIS VICINITY. MORE THAN
10.000 SICK AND WOUNDED
CONFEDERATE SOLDIERS RECEIVED
NECESSARY MEDICAL ATTENTION
WITHIN ITS WALLS DURING THE THREE
YEARS IT WAS OPERATED.

DEPARTMENT
OF NATURAL
RESOURCES

DIVISION OF
STATE PARKS
HISTORIC SITES
& MONUMENTS.

The Georgia state seal is engraved at the bottom of the slab.

See the entry for Union Point (Greene County) for a brief discussion of wayside homes.

Bibb County, Macon

LOCATION: Cotton Avenue and Second Street		DATE: 1879
STYLE: Statue of a soldier on a column		BUILDER: LMA
FABRICATOR: Muldoon Monument Company (McKenney)		

ERECTED A.D. 1879
BY THE
LADIES MEMORIAL ASSOCIATION OF MACON
IN HONOR OF
THE MEN OF BIBB COUNTY
AND OF ALL WHO GAVE THEIR LIVES TO THE
SOUTH TO ESTABLISH THE INDEPENDENCE OF THE
CONFEDERATE STATES.
1861–1865.

WITH PRIDE IN THEIR PATRIOTISM
WITH LOVE FOR THEIR MEMORY,
THIS SILENT STONE IS RAISED,
A PERPETUAL WITNESS OF OUR GRATITUDE.

The monument is located in a small triangular park, facing northeast. The original location was the wide median of Mulberry Street near Second Street. The author possesses a postcard showing the courthouse at that intersection, with the statue visible in the foreground.

The monument is 37 feet high, with the statue itself standing 10 1/2 feet. The monument cost $4,500. The statue and base are made of Cararra marble. It was moved to the current location in 1956 (McKenney).

Decorative elements include the Great Seal of the Confederacy and the Georgia Coat of Arms. There is also a carving in high relief depicting two flags (one with a broken staff), rifles with bayonets, a pile of cannon balls, and a scene of battle wreckage.

The soldier is standing at rest.

Bibb County, Macon

LOCATION: Median of Poplar Street at First Street | **DATE:** 1911

STYLE: Statues at base of an obelisk

BUILDERS: The husbands, fathers, sons, and daughters of the women of the South

"ERECTED TO THE MEMORY
OF THE WOMEN OF THE
SOUTH
BY THEIR HUSBANDS, FATHERS,
SONS AND DAUGHTERS."

There are two sets of statues at the base of the shaft. One set depicts a young matron with a child at her knee. On the opposite side of the obelisk is the same lady, giving drink to a wounded soldier.

As the statues tell a story, so do the two scenes carved on the plinth in bas relief. One shows a woman standing in the road in front of a farmhouse, watching as her man leaves for war. In the second scene, war and its misery have come to Georgia. The farmhouse is aflame. The detritus of battle litters the landscape. Armed men crouch in readiness.

CSA monograms are carved on all four sides of the obelisk. The dates of the war appear above one of the bas reliefs.

The monument was dedicated June 3, 1911. Its original location was just 100 yards away, in front of city hall. It was moved in 1934 when city hall was being renovated in a WPA project (McKenney).

The obelisk and statues are made of Georgia marble; the base is granite (Buzzett).

Bleckley County, Cochran

LOCATION: In front of old school, on North Second Street, adjacent to courthouse		
DATE: 1910	**STYLE**: Statue of a soldier on a column	**BUILDER**: UDC
FABRICATOR: McNeel Marble Co. (McNeel Memorials)		

IN MEMORY OF
OUR
CONFEDERATE
SOLDIERS

ERECTED BY THE
COCHRAN CHAPTER
NO. 764 U.D.C.
TO THE
CONFEDERATE VETERANS
OF PULASKI COUNTY, 1910.

"WHEN THE LAST TRUMPET
IS SOUNDED, MAY EACH ONE
ANSWER THE ROLL CALL OF
THE HEAVENLY ARMY."

The source of this quote is unknown. On the front of the plinth a cannon barrel protrudes between crossed sabers. On the opposite surface are crossed rifles and the remnant of a lost cannon barrel. Crossed flags and the dates of the war decorate the front of the column.

The monument was originally at the intersection of Beech Street and Second Street. It was moved in 1935 to the present location. The cannon barrel originally served as a waterspout, filling a horse trough. Built at a cost of $2,250, the monument was dedicated April 26, 1910 (McKenney).

In 1910 Cochran was in Pulaski County. Bleckley County was formed in 1912.

The soldier is standing at rest.

GEORGIA'S CONFEDERATE MONUMENTS

Brantley County, Waynesville

LOCATION: Mineral Springs Road, east of Browntown Road	DATE: 1906
STYLE: Obelisk and a memorial wall	BUILDER: UDC

ERECTED 1906
TO OUR
CONFEDERATE DEAD.
JESUP CHAPTER U.D.C.
1861–1865

Waynesville is on US Highway 82 between Brunswick and Waycross. It was the first seat of Wayne County, established in 1829. Brantley County was formed in 1920 from parts of Wayne and two other counties. By the latter part of the nineteenth century, Jesup was the main town in the area. It is unclear why the ladies in Jesup built the monument in Waynesville, 35 miles away.

This monument is not listed in Buzzett, McKenney, or Widener. It does appear in Wiggins and UDC 2002.

The long-neglected cemetery in which the obelisk is located was cleared in the late 1990s. The obelisk was placed on a stable foundation. In 2001, Confederate Soldiers Park was dedicated. The memorial wall made of brick was completed in 2005 (Wiggins).

The wall contains 150 marble inlays, most of which name Confederate soldiers, from local enlisted men to the most famous leaders of the Confederate armies. Some of the inlays credit the people who were involved in building the wall. One honors Jack Gibson, a private in Company A of the 4th Georgia Cavalry, identified as a "colored soldier."

Crossed battle flags decorate one side of the obelisk. Opposite the flags are crossed rifles.

Brooks County, Quitman

LOCATION: Courthouse grounds, East Screven Street (US Highway 84)

DATE: 1879 (McKenney) | STYLE: Obelisk | BUILDER: LMA

FABRICATOR: Ritter & Sons (McKenney)

OUR
CONFEDERATE DEAD.
ERECTED
BY THE LADIES
MEMORIAL ASSOCIATION
1878.

BROTHERS!
REST IN PEACE.

Brooks County, Quitman

LOCATION: West End Cemetery, East Screven Street (US Highway 84) and South Laurel Street		
DATE: 1936	STYLE: Memorial stone	BUILDERS: LMA and UDC

TO THE MEMORY OF
OUR UNKNOWN CONFEDERATE DEAD
DONATED BY
THE LADIES MEMORIAL ASSOCIATION
ERECTED BY
QUITMAN, GEORGIA, CHAPTER UNITED
DAUGHTERS OF THE CONFEDERACY
1936

According to a Georgia Historical Commission marker, erected in 1956, in the last year of the war a number of known and unknown Confederate soldiers were buried in this cemetery. Memorial services were held starting in 1869. On Confederate Memorial Day in 1871, a group of war orphans from Mississippi participated in the service. One of the orphan girls discovered that day that her father was among the dead buried in West End Cemetery.

Bryan County, Richmond Hill

LOCATION: J. F. Gregory Park, Cedar Street	**DATE:** 1980s (brochure for J. F. Gregory Park)
STYLE: Equestrian statue of Robert E. Lee	**BUILDER:** Ghaith R. Pharaon (UDC 2002)

ROBERT E. LEE

This statue, carved in Italy, was originally located at the nearby Henry Ford Plantation, which was owned by Ghaith Pharaon when he commissioned the statue. When Pharaon sold the plantation, the new owners donated the statue to the city. The monument was placed at its current location on January 1, 2000. It was valued at $35,000 at the time (Savannah Morning News, January 1, 2000; SavannahNow website, accessed June 2012). The statue is made of marble.

GEORGIA'S CONFEDERATE MONUMENTS

Bulloch County, Statesboro

LOCATION: Courthouse grounds, facing East Main Street	**DATE:** 1909
STYLE: Statue of a soldier on a column	**BUILDER:** UDC
FABRICATOR: McNeel Marble Co. (McNeel Memorials)	

ERECTED BY
THE STATESBORO CHAPTER
UNITED DAUGHTERS OF
THE CONFEDERACY
NUMBER 1100
APRIL 26, 1909

IN MEMORY OF
THE
CONFEDERATE SOLDIERS
1861–1865

COMRADES

"HOW MANY A GLORIOUS
NAME FOR US,
HOW MANY A STORY OF
FAME FOR US,
THEY LEFT: WOULD IT
NOT BE A BLAME FOR US,
IF THEIR MEMORIES PART
FROM OUR LAND AND HEART,
AND A WRONG TO THEM
AND A SHAME TO US?"

(From "C.S.A." by Abram J. Ryan, with a slight misquote)

According to McKenney, the cost is uncertain, one source giving a figure of $2,000 and another $4,200. McKenney quotes the poem correctly, not as incorrectly quoted on the monument itself. The final words should be "shame for us," not "shame to us."

A battle flag on the front of the column is loosely draped around its staff, and the soldier is standing at rest.

The monument is made entirely of marble.

Burke County, Waynesboro

LOCATION: Waynesboro Confederate Memorial Cemetery, West Sixth Street	

DATE: 1877 (McKenney)	**STYLE:** Obelisk	**BUILDER:** LMA

FABRICATOR: Theodore Markwalter (CSMA, p. 162)

ERECTED BY THE
LADIES MEMORIAL
ASSOCIATION OF
BURKE COUNTY.

APRIL 26,
1877.

These inscriptions are on the shaft at the base. The following inscriptions, including the duplicative one, are all on marble shields affixed to the shaft.

TO THE
CONFEDERATE DEAD,
WHO FELL IN THE
STRUGGLE FOR THE
"LOST CAUSE."
1861–1865.

THEY WHO DIE
FOR THEIR
COUNTRY,
FILL HONORED
GRAVES.

ERECTED BY THE
LADIES MEMORIAL
ASSOCIATION OF
BURKE COUNTY.

IN A COUNTRY'S
MEMORY
HER HEROES ARE
IMMORTAL.

The monument was originally located in the cemetery. It was moved downtown in 1899. The original cost was $375. During the move the height was raised from 15 feet to 21 feet, at a cost of $419.05 (CSMA, p. 163).

In the early 1950s, the monument was returned to the cemetery (McKenney). The author has an undated postcard with a picture of monument and courthouse. The automobiles in the picture date to the late 1920s or early 1930s.

GEORGIA'S CONFEDERATE MONUMENTS

Butts County, Jackson

LOCATION: Courthouse grounds, facing Third Street and South Oak Street		
DATE: 1911	**STYLE:** Statue of a soldier on a low pedestal	**BUILDER:** UDC
	FABRICATOR: McNeel Marble Co. (McKenney)	

ERECTED BY
LARKIN D. WATKINS
CHAPTER,
UNITED DAUGHTERS
OF THE CONFEDERACY
OF BUTTS COUNTY,
1911.

IN MEMORY OF THE
CONFEDERATE SOLDIERS
OF BUTTS COUNTY,
WHOSE UNDYING DEVOTION
TO DUTY AND SELF SACRIFICE
IN THEIR COUNTRY'S
SERVICE, WE CHERISH;
AND WHOSE HEROIC DEEDS
AND PATRIOTISM, WE EMBALM
IN STONE, AS THEY ARE
ENSHRINED IN OUR HEARTS.

OUR HEROES

"LEST WE FORGET."

The cost of the monument was $1,940 (McKenney).
The pedestal is decorated with crossed sabers and a flag. The dates of the war are inscribed on the panel with the flag. The soldier is in the order arms position.

Carroll County, Carrollton

LOCATION: Courthouse grounds, Newnan Street	DATE: 1910
STYLE: Statue of a soldier on a column	BUILDER: UDC
FABRICATOR: McNeel Marble Co. (McNeel Memorials)	

ERECTED
BY THE
ANNIE WHEELER CHAPTER
UNITED DAUGHTERS
OF THE CONFEDERACY
APRIL 26, 1910

UPON THE ALTAR
OF HOME AND COUNTRY,
THEY PLACED THE OFFERING
IN FULLEST MEASURE,
OF ALL THEY HAD TO GIVE.

IN PROUD AND LOVING
MEMORY OF THE
CONFEDERATE SOLDIERS
OF CARROLL COUNTY,
1861–1865

CONFEDERATE
DEAD

The following are lines from each of the two stanzas of "An Ode Written in the Beginning of the Year 1746," by William Collins, an eighteenth-century English poet. The quote contains the first two lines of the poem's first stanza and the first four of the second. The poem is also quoted on the Clay County monument.

"HOW SLEEP THE BRAVE,
WHO SINK TO REST,
BY ALL THEIR COUNTRY'S
WISHES BLEST!
BY FAIRY HANDS, THEIR
KNELL IS RUNG;
BY FORMS UNSEEN, THEIR
DIRGE IS SUNG;
THERE HONOR COMES, A
PILGRIM GRAY;
TO BLESS THE TURF
THAT WRAPS THEIR CLAY."

The original location was in the in the public square, facing north. In the 1950s, the square was eliminated. The monument was moved first to the hospital grounds then to the courthouse. The dedication was May 28, 1910 (McKenney).

The date of the first move was 1958, the second 1976 (Wiggins).

The soldier is standing at rest.

Carroll County, Carrollton

LOCATION: Veterans Memorial Park, Newnan Road	**DATE:** 2004 (Wiggins)
STYLE: Memorial wall	**BUILDER:** SCV (Wiggins)

"KIA"

"DEDICATED TO THE MEMORY OF THOSE
WHO DIED IN DEFENSE OF FREEDOM"

WAR BETWEEN THE STATES

Listed on this wall are the names of 143 Carroll County men killed in the war. A count of the surnames indicates that seventeen families suffered more than one death.

This wall is one element in a memorial to the county's dead in all wars. This element was the work of the McDaniel-Curtis Camp 165 of the Sons of Confederate Veterans (Wiggins).

Catoosa County, Ringgold

	LOCATION: Ringgold Gap Buttfield Park

DATE: 2009	STYLE: Bronze statue of General Patrick R. Cleburne on a stone pedestal

BUILDER: Pat Cleburne Society (*Atlanta Journal-Constitution*, December 28, 2008)

SCULPTOR: Ron Tunison

CLEBURNE

This photo was taken on October 3, 2009, at the unveiling of the statue. The Ringgold Telephone Company made a major contribution to support the project (Atlanta Journal-Constitution, *December 28, 2008).*

GEORGIA'S CONFEDERATE MONUMENTS

Chatham County, Savannah

LOCATION: Forsyth Park	**DATE:** 1875 (CSMA, p. 157)
STYLE: Bronze soldier on top of a large sandstone monument	
BUILDER: LMA (McKenney)	**FABRICATOR:** Montreal Marble Works
SCULPTOR: Sandstone monument—Robert Reid; bronze statue—David Richards (McKenney)	

TO THE
CONFEDERATE DEAD
1861–1865

"COME FROM THE FOUR WINDS, O BREATH,
AND BREATHE UPON THESE SLAIN, THAT THEY MAY LIVE"

(Ezekiel, 37:9, King James Version)

This monument is the work of the Ladies' Memorial Association of Chatham County. It was designed by Robert Reid and constructed by the Montreal Marble Works. The cornerstone was laid June 16, 1874. The dedication was held on May 24, 1875. A marble statue of the goddess Judgement originally topped the large sandstone edifice, and lower down, in a cupola, was the goddess Silence. These statues were soon removed and the cupola enclosed. Judgement was replaced by the soldier, who has stood since 1879. The re-dedication was held in May 1879 (McKenney).

This ornate monument is one of the very few in Georgia containing an inscription identifying the artist. There are two inscriptions on bronze tablets.

Silence is now in Laurel Grove Cemetery in Savannah. Judgement is in Thomasville's Laurel Hill Cemetery.

This monument is busy with decorations of all kinds: battlefield debris, cannonballs, drums, bugles, swords, flags, wreaths, fasces, and a female figure reclining under a tree.

Chatham County, Savannah

LOCATION: Catholic Cemetery, Wheaton Street	**DATE:** 1910 (McKenney)
STYLE: Bronze statue of a soldier on a low pedestal	
FABRICATOR: Oglethorpe Marble & Granite Co.	

IN MEMORY OF

THE

IRISH JASPER GREENS

COS. A AND B

FIRST VOL. REG. OF GEORGIA

WHO DIED IN THE SERVICE OF

THE CONFEDERATE STATES

1861–1865.

REQUIESCANT IN PACE.

IRISH JASPER GREENS

OGLE. M. & G. CO.

GEO. B. LITTLE MGR.

SAV. GA.

The statue was dedicated April 26, 1910, in the section of the cemetery where twenty-eight of the men of the companies are buried (Wiggins).

The soldier is leaning on his rifle. He is not erect: rather he slouches forward in a way that suggests he is wearied by the trials of war.

Chatham County, Savannah

LOCATION: Laurel Grove Cemetery, West Anderson Street	**DATE:** 1875 (Widener)
STYLE: A statue of the goddess Silence	**BUILDER:** LMA

TO THE
CONFEDERATE DEAD

HERE REST "TIL ROLL CALL"
THE MEN OF GETTYSBURG

ON FAME'S ETERNAL CAMPING GROUND
THEIR SILENT TENTS ARE SPREAD,
AND GLORY GUARDS, WITH SILENT ROUND
THE BIVOUAC OF THE DEAD.

(From "Bivouac of the Dead" by Theodore O'Hara)

TREAD LIGHTLY FOR EACH MAN BEQUEATHED
ERE PLACED BENEATH THIS SOD,
HIS ASHES TO HIS NATIVE LAND
HIS GALLANT SOUL TO GOD.

(From "The Soldier's Grave" by Pearl Rivers)

A statue of the goddess Silence, originally atop the monument in Forsyth Park

Chatham County, Savannah

LOCATION: Laurel Grove Cemetery, West Anderson Street		
DATE: 1875 (Widener)	**STYLE:** Obelisk	**BUILDER:** UCV

SLEEP
COMRADES

McLAWS CAMP
596, U.C.V.

Battle flags decorate each side of the obelisk.

Chatham County, Savannah

LOCATION: Laurel Grove Cemetery, West Anderson Street	DATE: 1872 (Widener)
STYLE: Memorial stone	BUILDER: Confederate Veterans Association

CONFEDERATE VETERANS ASSOCIATION OF SAVANNAH GA.
IN MEMORIAM

A marker at the foot of the stone states that it served as the base for a cannon that was removed in 1990 to Fort Jackson, on loan and for proper preservation. It is stipulated that the cannon is to be returned if public viewing at Fort Jackson is discontinued.

The marker is in a section of the cemetery containing Confederate graves.

Chattahoochee County, Cusseta

LOCATION: Courthouse grounds, Broad Street	**DATE:** Post 1931 (McKenney)
STYLE: Memorial stone with a bronze tablet	**BUILDER:** UDC

IN MEMORY OF
CONFEDERATE VETERANS
OF
CHATTAHOOCHEE COUNTY
1861–1865
UNITED DAUGHTERS CONFEDERACY

The UDC chapter was chartered in 1931, so the monument was built sometime after that date (McKenney).

Chattooga County, Menlo

LOCATION: Lawrence Park, facing Bell Street	**DATE:** 1915
STYLE: Cast iron statue of a soldier on a column	**BUILDER:** A. J. Lawrence

CHICKAMAUGA

VICKSBURG

BAKERS CREEK

LOOKOUT MOUNTAIN

ERECTED BY
A.J. LAWRENCE,
A.D. 1915
[50 YEARS AFTER
THE EVENT AT
APPOMATTOX],
AS A TRIBUTE TO THE
WOMEN WHO KEPT THE
HOMES AND PRAYED
BY THE FIRESIDES,
1861–1865.
THEIR WORK IS DONE,
THEIR PRAYERS ARE
ANSWERED.
AMEN.

THIS PARK
IS DONATED BY
THE FOUNDER OF
MENLO AS A
PLAYGROUND FOR
THE CHILDREN OF
THE GENERATIONS,
FOREVER.

TO THE PRIVATE
SOLDIER OF THE 60'S.
YOUR NAME AND
FAME SHALL NEVER
DIE AS LONG AS TIME
HER RECORD KEEPS.
NO FROST, NOR BLIGHT,
NOR WITHERING WIND,
DISTURBS YOUR LAST
LONG SLEEP.

On one surface of the plinth is the Masonic "square-and-compasses" symbol and the Scottish Rite date "A. M. 5919." The soldier is standing at rest.

Lawrence was a local man whose family had divided loyalties in the Civil War. His brother, John Milton Lawrence, was killed fighting in the Union army. Jack Lawrence served briefly in Company D of the 34th Georgia. He deserted, took a loyalty oath, and lived in the North until the end of the war. He returned home after the war and lived in Chattooga County until his death.

The roster of Company D, the comrades Lawrence deserted, is listed on the column.

Cherokee County, Canton

LOCATION: Brown Park, Elizabeth Street

DATE: 1923 | STYLE: Marble arch | BUILDER: UDC

DEDICATED
IN LOVING
REMEMBRANCE
APRIL 26 1923

ERECTED BY
HELEN PLANE
CHAPTER ~ UNITED
DAUGHTERS OF THE
CONFEDERACY

IN MEMORY OF
OUR SOUTHERN
HEROES OF THE
WAR BETWEEN
THE STATES

IN HONOR OF
OUR BOYS WHO
FOUGHT IN THE
WORLD WAR

THEIR NAMES MAY
BE FORGOTTEN BUT
THEIR DEEDS ARE
RECORDED IN THE
ANNALS OF THEIR
GRATEFUL COUNTRY

After the next great conflict the dual-purpose arch was given a third purpose.

IN MEMORY OF
OUR HEROES OF
WORLD WAR II
1941–1945

On one side of the arch the keystone bears the dates "1861–1865." Confederate Confederate Battle Flags flank the dates. The opposite side has the dates 1917–1918 and the Stars and Stripes.

This is one of the few memorials to the soldiers of the Confederacy and to local men who fought in the United States army in World War I.

Clarke County, Athens

LOCATION: Broad Street		**DATE:** 1871
STYLE: Marble column	**BUILDER:** LMA	**FABRICATOR:** Markwalter

TO OUR
CONFEDERATE
DEAD.

IN A COUNTRY'S
MEMORY,
HER BRAVE
ARE IMMORTAL.

BRIGHT ANGELS
COME
AND GUARD OUR
SLEEPING
HEROES.

ERECTED
BY THE
LADIES'
MEMORIAL
ASSOCIATION.
1871.

"FAITH IN GOD" is inscribed inside a wreath, between crossed rifles and flags.

CONFEDERATE DEAD
OF ATHENS, GA.

CONFEDERATE DEAD
OF CLARKE CO., GA.

Under these two headings are lists of names, nearly 200 in all.

TRUE TO THE SOIL
THAT GAVE THEM BIRTH
AND REARED THEM MEN;
TRUE TO THEIR
ANCESTORS OF HIGH
RENOWN
AND HALLOWED WORTH;
CHERISHING THE
SENTIMENTS OF HOME
AND COUNTRY
AND THE ALLEGIANCE
THEREUNTO DUE
AS ONE AND
INSEPARABLE:
THESE HEROES—OURS IN
THE UNITY OF BLOOD
OURS IN THE UNITY OF
PATRIOTISM
STRUGGLED FOR THE
RIGHTS OF STATES
AS HELD BY THE FATHERS

OF THE REPUBLIC
AND BY THE FATHERS AS
A SACRED TRUST
UNTO THEM,
BEQUEATHED.
THE MEASURE OF THEIR
YEARS SUDDENLY
COMPLETED
IN THE FATAL ISSUES OF
BATTLE,
REACHED THE
CONSUMMATION OF
EARTHLY GLORY
BY THEIR DEATH.
LAST AND HOLIEST
OFFICE OF HUMAN
FIDELITY
POSSIBLE TO BRAVE MEN.
ATTESTING THEIR
SINCERITY, PROVING
THEIR HONOR,
AND SEALING THEIR
INTEGRITY
THEY WON THEIR TITLE TO
AN IMMORTALITY
OF LOVE AND
REVERENCE.

The monument was originally located at College Street and Washington Street at a cost of $4,444. Later it was moved to city hall. Its present location is its third home (McKenney). The inscription was written by Reverend Andrew A. Lipscomb (Buzzett, citing Mildred Rutherford). Lipscomb was president of the University of Georgia from 1860–1874. The column is suggestive of church spire.

Clarke County, Athens

LOCATION: Oconee Hill Cemetery	**DATE:** 1897 (Marshall, pp. 124, 502)
STYLE: Obelisk	**BUILDER:** UDC (Marshall, pp. 124, 501)
FABRICATOR: Peter Bisson & Sons Classic City Granite Works (Marshall, pp. 124, 501-502)	

OUR

UNKNOWN

HEROES

1861–1865

Marshall cites articles (Athens Banner, April 9 and 30, 1897) that discuss the construction of the monument and the services held on Confederate Memorial Day of that year. The granite obelisk replaced an earlier tin monument that had stood at the cemetery's entrance.

The newspaper credits the "Athens Chapter, Daughters of the Confederacy" as the builder, without specific reference to the UDC. The Laura Rutherford Chapter of the UDC was chartered in 1896 and was certainly the organization responsible for the work.

Clay County, Fort Gaines

LOCATION: New Park Cemetery	**DATE:** 1907
STYLE: Small stone column	**BUILDER:** UDC

SACRED TO THE
MEMORY OF
THE
CONFEDERATE
DEAD
BURIED WITHIN
OUR GATES.
ERECTED BY THE
LODGE OF THE
U. D. C. OF FT. GAINES
1907

HOW SLEEP THE BRAVE
WHO SINK TO REST,
BY ALL THEIR COUNTRY'S
WISHES BLEST.

*(From "An Ode Written in the Beginning
of the Year 1746" by William Collins)*

The obelisk is in a section of the cemetery containing graves of unknown Confederates.

Clayton County, Jonesboro

LOCATION: Pat Cleburne Cemetery	**DATE:** 1934

STYLE: Stone arch at the entrance to the cemetery; memorial stone in the center

BUILDER: LMA	**FABRICATOR:** Enterprise Marble & Granite Co.

On the arch:
"CONFEDERATE DEAD" IS INSCRIBED
ON THE KEYSTONE.

One the left abutment:
ERECTED BY
THE ATLANTA LADIES
MEMORIAL ASSOCIATION
OF ATLANTA GA.
APRIL 1934

MRS. ARTHUR McDERMOTTE
WILSON, JR.
PRESIDENT

On the right abutment:
COMMITTEE
MRS. ERNEST B. WILLIAMS
MRS. JOHN MORELAND SPEER
MRS. CHARLES J. HADEN
MRS. G. H. BRANDON
MRS. JOHN L. HARPER

"LOVE MAKES MEMORY
ETERNAL."

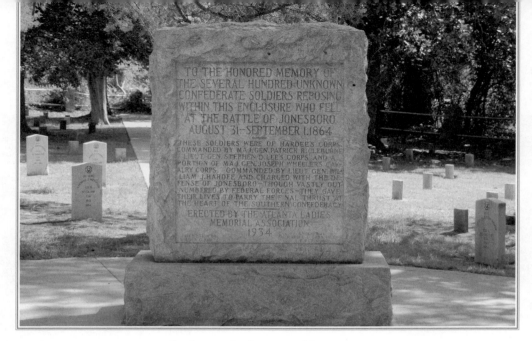

On the stone in the center of the cemetery:

TO THE HONORED MEMORY OF
THE SEVERAL HUNDRED UNKNOWN
CONFEDERATE SOLDIERS REPOSING
WITHIN THIS ENCLOSURE WHO FELL
AT THE BATTLE OF JONESBORO
AUGUST 31–SEPTEMBER 1, 1864

THESE SOLDIERS WERE OF HARDEE'S CORPS,
COMMANDED BY MAJ. GEN. PATRICK R. CLEBURNE
LIEUT. GEN. STEPHEN D. LEE'S CORPS AND A
PORTION OF MAJ. GEN. JOSEPH WHEELER'S CAV-
ALRY CORPS. COMMANDED BY LIEUT. GEN. WIL-
LIAM J. HARDEE AND CHARGED WITH THE DE-
FENSE OF JONESBORO—THOUGH VASTLY OUT-
NUMBERED BY FEDERAL FORCES—THEY GAVE
THEIR LIVES TO PARRY THE FINAL THRUST AT
THE HEART OF THE SOUTHERN CONFEDERACY

ERECTED BY THE ATLANTA LADIES
MEMORIAL ASSOCIATION
1934

At the bottom of the stone, the author of the inscription and the fabricator are named:

INSCRIPTION BY
WILBUR G. KURTZ
ENTERPRISE
MARBLE & GRANITE CO.
E. E. REDD MGR.

Clayton County, Lovejoy

LOCATION: Tara Boulevard, north of McDonough Road		**DATE:** 1939	
STYLE: Marble Sigma Chi cross		**BUILDER:** Sigma Chi Fraternity	

On one of several bronze tablets:

ERECTED BY THE SIGMA CHI
FRATERNITY IN MEMORY
OF ITS CONSTANTINE CHAPTER
ORGANIZED HEREABOUTS ON
SEPTEMBER 17, 1864, THAT SIGMA CHI
SHOULD NOT PERISH IN THE SOUTH.
SEPTEMBER 17, 1939

Bronze tablets tell in some detail the story of Harry S. Dixon and other members of the fraternity, all serving in a Mississippi regiment, who met here after the fall of Atlanta to form the Constantine Chapter of the Sigma Chi Fraternity. According to one of the tablets, the marble cross and its foundation weigh 105 tons.

Cobb County, Marietta

LOCATION: Confederate Cemetery, Powder Springs Street		**DATE:** 1908
STYLE: Obelisk	**BUILDER:** UDC	**FABRICATOR:** McNeel Marble Co. (McNeel Memorials)

TO OUR
CONFEDERATE DEAD.

ERECTED AND
DEDICATED, BY
KENNESAW CHAPTER,
UNITED DAUGHTERS
OF THE
CONFEDERACY,
MARIETTA, GEORGIA.
1908.

Above the dedication is the UDC insignia.

TO THE
3000 SOLDIERS IN THIS
CEMETERY, FROM EVERY
SOUTHERN STATE, WHO
FELL ON GEORGIA SOIL,
IN DEFENSE OF GEORGIA
RIGHTS AND GEORGIA
HOMES.

"THEY SLEEP THE SLEEP OF OUR
NOBLE SLAIN,
DEFEATED, YET WITHOUT A STAIN,
PROUDLY AND PEACEFULLY."

*(These are the slightly altered final lines
of "The Sword of Robert Lee"
by Abram J. Ryan.)*

*On the opposite surface is the
Southern Cross of Honor. Beneath the cross
is the following inscription:*

TO OUR COBB COUNTY
SOLDIERS, WHO SO NOBLY
"ILLUSTRATED" GEORGIA, ON
MANY A HARD WON FIELD;
TO THOSE WHO DIED FOR
A SACRED CAUSE AND TO
THOSE WHO LIVED TO
WIN A NOBLER VICTORY,
IN TIME OF PEACE.

*On another surface, beneath a
Confederate Battle Flag is a quote from Ryan's
"The Conquered Banner."*

"FOR THOUGH CONQUERED,
THEY ADORE IT
LOVE THE COLD DEAD HANDS
THAT BORE IT."

*The monument is 25 feet tall, and made of Elbert County granite (McKenney).
McKenney attributes the monument's construction to the ladies' memorial association as
well as to the UDC, but the monument's inscriptions do not mention the LMA.*

Cobb County, Marietta

LOCATION: Confederate Cemetery, Powder Springs Street	DATE: 1911
STYLE: Marble gateway	
FABRICATOR: McNeel Marble Co. (*Marietta Daily Journal*, December 15, 1911)	

CONFEDERATE CEMETERY

(This is inscribed on each face of the lintel.)

ERECTED

A.D. 1911.

The gateway is placed on a walk down the hill from the obelisk, at the point at which a pedestrian approaching from the north enters the area containing Confederate graves. This edifice is often described as an arch, but structurally it is composed of two columns spanned by a lintel. The Marietta Daily Journal *reported on December 15, 1911, that McNeel had completed the "arch" that week at a cost of $1,400.*

Cobb County, Marietta

LOCATION: Brown Park, West Atlanta Street, adjacent to the Confederate Cemetery	
DATE: 2012	**STYLE:** Bronze statue of mother and child
BUILDER: City of Marietta (*Marietta Daily Journal*, April 16, 2012)	
SCULPTORS: T. J. Dixon and James Nelson (*Marietta Daily Journal*, April 16, 2012)	

"THE SOUTH LAID HER BEST UPON THE ALTAR OF HER COUNTRY."
MATTIE HARRIS LYON

This statue was unveiled on April 15, 2012. The unveiling was performed by Marietta Mayor Steve Tumlin and former Councilwoman Betty Hunter. Mattie Harris Lyon was a long-time leader in Marietta, active in civic affairs throughout her long life.

Henry Sinclair was the model for the statue of the boy. The cost of the statues was $75,000 (conversation with Betty Hunter, May 2012).

Cobb County, Marietta

LOCATION: Brown Park, West Atlanta Street, adjacent to the Confederate Cemetery	
DATE: 2009	**STYLE:** Two memorial walls; pair of bronze boots on a granite base
BUILDERS: Marietta Confederate Cemetery Foundation and Friends of Brown Park (conversation with Betty Hunter, May 2012)	
FABRICATOR: Bob Greenway (conversation with Greenway, April 2012)	

"THIS IS NOT A CEMETERY
OF GRAVES, BUT A
RARE GARDEN OF HEROES."

GENERAL CLEMENT A. EVANS, JULY 7, 1908

* * * * *

*Between the walls is a granite block on which rest a pair of bronze boots.
The inscription on the base reads:*

IN
MEMORY OF
THE UNKNOWN
SOLDIERS BURIED
IN THE MARIETTA
CONFEDERATE
CEMETERY

The granite walls contain the names of all the known dead and (for most) their states. There is a map showing the sites of the battles in North Georgia where many fell. One panel contains a chronology of key events in the history of the cemetery from its foundation in 1863 to 1989, when the remains of an unknown Confederate, long buried at Cheatham Hill where he fell, were reinterred.

One panel of the wall contains a list of donors. The cost of the wall was approximately $70,000 (conversation with Betty Hunter, June 2012).

Cobb County, Kennesaw

LOCATION: Beaumont Drive, on top of Pine Mountain	**DATE**: 1902
STYLE: Memorial stone	**BUILDERS**: J. Gid and Mary J. Morris

1861. 1865.

IN MEMORY OF
LIEUT. GEN. LEONIDAS
POLK

WHO FELL ON THIS SPOT
JUNE 14. 1864.

FOLDING HIS ARMS ACROSS HIS
BREAST
HE STOOD GAZING ON THE
SCENES BELOW,
TURNING HIMSELF AROUND AS IF
TO TAKE A FAREWELL VIEW.

THUS STANDING A CANNON SHOT
FROM THE ENEMY'S GUNS
CRASHED THROUGH HIS BREAST,
AND OPENED A WIDE DOOR
THROUGH WHICH HIS SPIRIT TOOK
ITS FLIGHT TO JOIN HIS COMRADES
ON THE OTHER SHORE.

SURELY THE EARTH NEVER
OPENED HER ARMS TO ALLOW THE
HEAD OF A BRAVER MAN TO REST
UPON HER BOSOM.

SURELY THE LIGHT NEVER PUSHED
THE DARKNESS BACK TO MAKE
BRIGHTER THE ROAD THAT LEADS
TO THE LAMB.

AND SURELY THE GATES OF HEAV-
EN NEVER OPENED WIDER TO
ALLOW A MORE MANLY SPIRIT TO
ENTER THEREIN.

ERECTED BY
J. GID & MARY J. MORRIS
1902.

On the opposite side of the stone:

NORTH

VENI VEDI VICI

WITH 5 TO 1

The monument is on the property of Fred D. Bentley, Sr. It is in good condition, but some thoughtless people have carved their initials on the stone and the base.

The word "SOUTH" is inscribed above a Confederate Battle Flag on the south side of the monument. Beneath the flag is the principal inscription.

Coffee County, Douglas

LOCATION: Courthouse grounds, facing Ward Street	**DATE:** 1911
STYLE: Statue of a soldier on a column	**BUILDER:** UDC
FABRICATOR: McNeel Marble Co. (McNeel Memorials)	

CSA

IN MEMORY OF
OUR
CONFEDERATE
SOLDIERS

ERECTED BY THE
ROBERT E. LEE
CHAPTER, U.D.C
OCT. 1911.

The dates of the war are inscribed above crossed battle flags.

The monument's original location was at the intersection of Ashley Street and Peterson Avenue. The cost was $1,200 (McKenney).

Wiggins contains a photograph of the monument, taken in 1911, showing the monument in the middle of the dirt street.

The soldier is standing at rest.

Colquitt County, Moultrie

LOCATION: Courthouse grounds, facing First Avenue	DATE: 1909
STYLE: Statue of a soldier on a column	BUILDER: UDC
FABRICATOR: McNeel Marble Co. (McNeel Memorials)	

ERECTED BY

MOULTRIE-McNEILL

CHAPTER OF

THE DAUGHTERS OF

THE CONFEDERACY.

MOULTRIE GEORGIA.

1909.

IN HONOR OF OUR

CONFEDERATE

DEAD.

"ON FAME'S ETERNAL

CAMPING GROUND,

THEIR SILENT TENTS

ARE SPREAD,

AND GLORY GUARDS

WITH SOLEMN ROUND,

THE BIVOUAC OF THE DEAD."

(From "The Bivouac of the Dead" by Theodore O'Hara)

"LEST WE FORGET."

COMRADES

The dates of the war are inscribed on pediments above the plinth, front and rear. "CSA" is inscribed on the adjacent pediments.

The monument was dedicated on April 23, 1909. At 35 feet, it is taller than is typical. The cost was approximately $5,000. Four stone cannonballs originally topped the corners of the base (McKenney).

Crossed rifles and flags decorate two sides of the plinth. The soldier is standing at rest.

Columbia County, Appling

LOCATION: Inside the old courthouse, Ray Owens Road (Georgia Highway 47)	
DATE: Before 1885 (McKenney)	STYLE: Tablet listing the county's war dead

OUR DEAD

The large central tablet lists the Columbia County men who lost their lives in the Civil War. The soldiers are listed by the companies in which they served. By the author's count there are 154 names. Smaller tablets on the sides name the men who died in World War I and World War II, totaling seventeen. This is located in the restored courtroom on the second floor of the old Columbia County Courthouse.

In nearby Thomson, in McDuffie County, there is a more typical Confederate monument, an obelisk that serves the dual purpose of honoring the Confederate dead of both McDuffie and Columbia counties.

The date of the Civil War tablet is unknown, but it is mentioned in a newspaper article in 1885 (McKenney).

UDC 2002 lists all the names on the tablets.

Columbia County, Evans

LOCATION: County office complex, Ronald Reagan Drive		
DATE: 2006	STYLE: Obelisk	BUILDER: SCV

THIS MONUMENT IS DEDICATED
TO ALL MEN FROM COLUMBIA COUNTY
WHO BRAVELY SERVED DURING THE
WAR BETWEEN THE STATES
1861–1865

ERECTED BY
THE MAJOR GENERAL
AMBROSE RANSOM WRIGHT
SONS OF CONFEDERATE VETERANS
CAMP # 1914
APRIL 26, 2006

* * * * *

COMPANY F
10TH GA. INFANTRY
"THOMSON GUARDS"

COMPANY K
16TH GA. INFANTRY
"RAMSEY VOLUNTEERS"

COMPANY H
37TH GA. INFANTRY
"'PETTUS VOLUNTEERS"

COMPANY K
48TH GA. INFANTRY
"HAMILTON RANGERS"

The names of four companies are listed on two sides of the plinth of polished black granite.

The other sides of the plinth display the First National Flag (with seven stars) and the Great Seal of the Confederacy. "CSA" is repeated on all four sides above the plinth.

GEORGIA'S CONFEDERATE MONUMENTS

Columbia County, Grovetown

LOCATION: Patriots Park, Columbia Road (Georgia Highway 232), east of Appling-Harlem Road		
DATE: Ca. 1992	**STYLE:** Memorial wall	**BUILDER:** Columbia County

THIS MONUMENT IS DEDICATED TO THE
CITIZENS OF COLUMBIA COUNTY
WHO ANSWERED THE CALL TO SERVE
THEIR COUNTRY AND IN SO DOING
MADE THE ULTIMATE SACRIFICE.

THE SONS AND DAUGHTERS OF COLUMBIA
COUNTY HAVE PROUDLY SERVED IN
CONFLICTS AROUND THE WORLD.

A list of wars follows this inscription, starting with the Revolutionary War and ending with the Persian Gulf War. The United States flag, in color, and the Great Seal of the United States top the center slab on the west side. The seals of the branches of service are also shown. The Iwo Jima statue and other famous works of art pertaining to different wars are carved in bas relief. Columbia County's war dead from World War I through Vietnam are shown on the west side, thirty-three in number.

The Georgia and Columbia County seals are on the east side. On this side are listed the county's dead in the War Between the States, numbering 160.

The information on the date and the builder was provided by Barry Smith, Columbia County's director of community and leisure services (conversation with Smith, June 2012).

Columbia County, Grovetown

LOCATION: Old Wrightsboro Road and East Robinson Avenue		**DATE:** 2007
STYLE: Memorial wall	**BUILDER:** City of Grovetown	
FABRICATOR: McCannon Granite Co., Elberton		
ARCHITECT: Johnson, Laschober & Assoc., Augusta		

GROVETOWN MEMORIAL PARK

I HAVE FOUGHT A GOOD FIGHT
I HAVE FINISHED MY COURSE
I HAVE KEPT THE FAITH

(2 Timothy 4:7, King James Version)

FEAR NOT THAT YE HAVE
DIED FOR NAUGHT
THE TORCH YE THREW
TO US WE CAUGHT
TEN MILLION HANDS WILL
HOLD IT HIGH
AND FREEDOM'S LIGHT
SHALL NEVER DIE!

*(From "America's Answer" by R. W. Lillard, one
of several poems written in reply to "In Flanders
Fields" by John McRae)*

The south side of the serpentine wall of polished granite contains the names of Columbia County's men and women who served in the forces of the United States in the wars of the twentieth and twenty-first centuries and in peacetime. There are separate sections for the Army, Navy, Air Force, and Marine Corps. For those veterans who served in wartime the name of the conflict is indicated.

Alongside the inscriptions is the seal of Grovetown. At each section of names are the seals of the branches of service.

The county's Confederate veterans are listed on the north side of the wall, where their names are carved along with the Great Seal of the Confederacy. There are 363 names in the Confederate section. Approximately twice that number are listed for all other conflicts and for service in time of peace.

The cost of the wall and related structures was approximately $280,000. Engraving the names alone cost $29,000, at a rate of $3.50 per character. Names will continue to be added as the county's men and women continue to serve.

The tablet in the courthouse in nearby Appling lists the county's Confederate dead, totaling 154, over 40 percent of the Confederate veterans listed in Grovetown.

The information on the date, the fabricator, the architect, and the estimate of the cost was provided by Dennis Trudeau (mayor of Grovetown, 1987–2007) and Shirley Beasley (city administrator) (conversations with Trudeau and Beasley, June 2012).

Coweta County, Newnan

LOCATION: Courthouse grounds, facing Jefferson Street		**DATE:** 1885	
STYLE: Statue of a soldier on a pedestal		**BUILDER:** LMA	
FABRICATOR: John Walton (McKenney)			

OUR CONFEDERATE DEAD,
WHOM POWER COULD NOT CORRUPT,
WHOM DEATH COULD NOT TERRIFY,
WHOM DEFEAT COULD NOT DISHONOR.

*(This is a variation of a passage from a speech by William Henry Trescot.
See the text for the Cartersville monument in Bartow County.)*

IT IS NOT IN MORTALS
TO COMMAND SUCCESS,
BUT THEY DID MORE,
DESERVED IT.

ERECTED 1885.

1861 1865

This monument was dedicated on December 29, 1885. The soldier is made of Italian marble and was carved in Italy. The monument is 22 feet tall in total, with the soldier himself accounting for 7'4". The cost was $2,000. Originally in a fenced enclosure in the street, facing south, the structure was moved ca. 1914 to the east side of courthouse (McKenney).

The soldier is standing at rest.

Coweta, Newnan

LOCATION: Oak Hill Cemetery, Bullsboro Road	STYLE: Memorial stone	BUILDER: LMA

OUR CONFEDERATE DEAD

NO CAUSE E'ER ROSE SO JUST AND TRUE,
NONE FELL SO FREE FROM CRIME.

*Beneath these lines are crossed flags, the Confederate Battle Flag
and a variation of the First National.*

ERECTED BY THE LADIES MEMORIAL ASSOCIATION TO THE
MEMORY OF OUR SOUTHERN HEROES WHO WORE THE GREY.
OUTNUMBERED NOT CONQUERED.

Adjacent to this monument is the grave of William Thomas Overby. (See the entry below for the Overby monument.) Overby was put to rest here in 1997, according to the inscription on the grave.

The flags on this memorial have a blue tint. Talbot County has the only one other monument in Georgia with this characteristic.

The dates of the war are inscribed in the upper right and left corners of the stone.

IN MEMORY OF
WILLIAM THOMAS OVERBY.
CONFEDERATE HERO.

ENLISTED MAY 31, 1861. Co. A, 7TH GA. INFANTRY.
WOUNDED AT SECOND MANASSAS AUG. 30, 1862.
THEN JOINED Co. D, 43RD BATLN. MOSBY'S RANGERS.

RAIDED WITHIN FEDERAL LINES TO EMBARRASS
ENEMY, CAUSING U.S. GRANT TO ISSUE ORDER,
"WHEN FOUND MOSBY'S MEN TO BE HANGED
WITHOUT TRIAL".

CAPTURED AT FRONT ROYAL, VA., FRIDAY SEPT. 23,
1864, OFFERED HIS LIFE TO REVEAL HIDING PLACE
OF MOSBY'S MEN. THIS HE REFUSED, AND WAS
EXECUTED WITHOUT TRIAL.

A FEDERAL SAID, "HE WAS THE NATHAN HALE OF
THE CONFEDERACY." SCOTT SAID, "HE WAS A
FAMOUS SOLDIER-AND DIED UNAFRAID". A LADY,
PRESENT AT HIS DEATH SAID, "HE DIED A
CHRISTIAN-UNAFRAID."

HE SUFFERED DEATH RATHER THAN BETRAY HIS
FRIENDS. BURIED AT MARKHAM, VA.
ERECTED
1956
BY ALFRED COLQUITT AND NEWNAN
CHAPTERS, UDC. INSCRIPTION BY
COL. THOMAS SPENCER.

Coweta County, Newnan

LOCATION: Courthouse grounds, facing Jackson Street	**DATE:** 1956
STYLE: Memorial stone	**BUILDER:** UDC

IN MEMORY OF
WILLIAM THOMAS OVERBY
CONFEDERATE HERO.

ENLISTED MAY 31, 1861, CO. A, 7TH GA. INFANTRY.
WOUNDED AT SECOND MANASSAS AUG. 30, 1862.
THEN JOINED CO. D, 43RD BATLN. MOSBY'S RANGERS.

RAIDED WITHIN FEDERAL LINES TO EMBARRASS
ENEMY, CAUSING U.S. GRANT TO ISSUE ORDER,
"WHEN FOUND MOSBY'S MEN TO BE HANGED
WITHOUT TRIAL."

CAPTURED AT FRONT ROYAL, VA., FRIDAY SEPT. 23,
1864. OFFERED HIS LIFE TO REVEAL HIDING PLACE
OF MOSBY'S MEN. THIS HE REFUSED, AND WAS
EXECUTED WITHOUT TRIAL.

A FEDERAL SAID, "HE WAS THE NATHAN HALE OF
THE CONFEDERACY." SCOTT SAID, "HE WAS A
FAMOUS SOLDIER—AND DIED UNAFRAID." A LADY,
PRESENT AT HIS DEATH SAID, "HE DIED A
CHRISTIAN—UNAFRAID."

HE SUFFERED DEATH RATHER THAN BETRAY HIS
FRIENDS. BURIED AT MARKHAM VA.

ERECTED
1956
BY ALFRED COLQUITT AND NEWNAN
CHAPTERS, UDC. INSCRIPTION BY
COL. THOMAS SPENCER.

In 1997 the remains of Sergeant Overby were removed from the Virginia burial ground and reinterred in Newnan's Oak Hill Cemetery. (See the entry above for Oak Hill Cemetery.) Above the inscriptions are crossed battle flags.

Crawford County, Roberta

LOCATION: Park at East Crusselle Street and Wright Avenue		
DATE: 2002	STYLE: Memorial wall	BUILDER: UDC

DEDICATED TO ALL
CRAWFORD COUNTY
VETERANS
WHO DIED IN SERVICE
TO OUR COUNTRY

THIS VETERANS WAR MEMORIAL WAS PLACED
MEMORIAL DAY 2002 AND
DEDICATED VETERANS DAY 2002
BY THE CRAWFORD COUNTY UDC 2562

UNITED DAUGHTERS OF THE CONFEDERACY ® CHAPTER 2562

*This is on a bronze tablet placed on the stone, above which is the
Great Seal of the Confederacy, also in bronze.*

The front of the monument contains the names of Crawford County's war dead. The center slab names the twenty-two Crawford County men killed in World War I, World War II, and Vietnam. The four larger flanking slabs list the men killed in the War between the States—256 in number.

"WAR BETWEEN THE STATES" is inscribed beneath the two slabs on the left and again on the right. Beneath the center slab are the names of the other wars.

All the inscriptions are on the rear of the monument.

GEORGIA'S CONFEDERATE MONUMENTS

Crisp County, Cordele

LOCATION: Grounds of the Community Clubhouse, Sixteenth Avenue (US Highway 280) and Seventh Street (US Highway 41)

DATE: 1911	STYLE: Statue of a soldier on a column	BUILDER: UDC

FABRICATOR: McNeel Marble Co. (McNeel Memorials)

1861–1865

THE
CONFEDERATE
PRIVATE SOLDIER.

ERECTED BY
CORDELE CHAPTER
No.793 U.D.C.

1911

"HE SPRANG INTO BATTLE-LINE TO
DEFEND HIS INVADED COUNTRY;
HE WON MARVELOUS VICTORIES;
HE SUFFERED NO DISCREDITABLE
DEFEAT;
HE NEVER ABUSED A TRIUMPH, AND
NEVER LOST FORTITUDE IN THE
HOUR OF DISASTER."

*(From an address made on Confederate
Memorial Day, 1893, by Colonel Charles C.
Jones, Jr., to the Confederate Survivors'
Association in Augusta [Jones, 27])*

"AMID THE CONFEDERATE LIGHTS
AND SHADOWS CAST UPON THE
HISTORIC CANVAS,
WE TRACE NO SEMBLANCE OF
DISHONOR, NO SUGGESTION OF
THOUGHT OR ACT
UNWORTHY OF THE LOFTIEST
ASPIRATION AND THE BRAVEST
ENDEAVOR."

(Source unknown)

There are four urns at the corners of the base. On the sides of the plinth are crossed cannon barrels (with a rammer) and crossed sabers. Garlands decorate all four sides of the plinth.

Work on the monument started in 1906. The height of 25 feet was claimed at time (incorrectly) to be the tallest south of Atlanta. The cost was $3,000. The monument was moved from its original location at 12th Avenue and Seventh Street because of traffic (McKenney).

The soldier is standing in the order arms position.

Dade County, Trenton

LOCATION: Park across Main Street from the courthouse	**DATE**: 2003
STYLE: Memorial wall	**BUILDERS**: SCV and the citizens of Dade County

The front contains the Great Seal of the Confederacy, the SCV logo and the following inscriptions:

DEDICATED TO THE SOLDIERS
AND FAMILIES
OF DADE COUNTY, GEORGIA
FOR THEIR SERVICE TO THE
CONFEDERATE STATES OF AMERICA
1861–1865.

"LEST WE FORGET"

IT IS A DUTY WE OWE
POSTERITY TO SEE THAT
OUR CHILDREN SHALL KNOW
THE VIRTUES AND BECOME WORTHY
OF THEIR SIRES.

THIS MONUMENT DEDICATED BY
THE SONS OF CONFEDERATE VETERANS
STATE OF DADE CAMP 707
AND THE CITIZENS OF DADE COUNTY

APRIL 26, 2003

FOUR YEARS ON THE FIRING LINE
COLONEL JAMES COOPER NISBET
66TH GEORGIA INFANTRY

On the sides are the names of men serving in two companies, Company B of the 6th Georgia Infantry Regiment (the Lookout Dragoons) and Company H of the 21st Georgia Infantry Regiment (the Silver Grays). The ranks of the officers and men are shown as well. There are 200 names.

On the rear of the wall are the names of more Dade County men, those serving in Company F of the 34th Georgia Infantry Regiment and Company D of the 39th (the Dade County Invincibles). These lists also show the ranks of the officers and men.

Each list numbers about 100 names. Also named are approximately fifty other Dade men who served in other military units. Also on the rear:

DEO VINDICE

ALTHOUGH DEFEATED,
THEY LEFT US TRADITIONS OF FAITH IN GOD,
HONOR, CHIVALRY AND RESPECT FOR WOMANHOOD;
THEY LEFT US A PASSIONATE BELIEF
IN FREEDOM FOR THE INDIVIDUAL.
OUR CONFEDERATE ANCESTORS BEQUEATHED TO US
A MILITARY TRADITION OF VALOR,
PATRIOTISM, DEVOTION TO DUTY
AND A SPIRIT OF SELF-SACRIFICE.
WHEN OUR NATION NO LONGER ADMIRES
AND PAYS TRIBUTE
TO THESE TRADITIONS,
WE WILL NO LONGER REMAIN
A FREE NATION.

The final inscription quotes from the initiation service for new members inducted into the Sons of Confederate Veterans. The rear has a map of the county at the top, between the words "STATE OF DADE" and the dates "1860–1945."

GEORGIA'S CONFEDERATE MONUMENTS

Dawson County, Dawsonville

LOCATION: Veterans Memorial Park, Georgia Highway 9, north of town

DATE: 2007 (This is the likely date, the year the park was re-named Veterans Memorial Park.)

STYLE: Memorial wall

In the center:

DAWSON COUNTY WAR MEMORIAL

WE, THE FUTURE GENERATION OF
PROUD DAWSON COUNTIANS DEDICATE
THIS MEMORIAL TO THE BRAVE MEN
AND WOMEN OF OUR COUNTY WHO SO
UNSELFISHLY GAVE OF THEMSELVES
SO THAT OTHERS MAY LIVE AND
ENJOY FREEDOM.
IT IS SAID, "WHAT YOU ARE IS
GOD'S GIFT TO YOU; WHAT YOU
BECOME IS YOUR GIFT TO GOD."
THROUGH THE EFFORTS OF ALL THESE
VETERANS, WE HAVE THE OPPORTUNITY
TO BECOME ALL THAT WE CAN BE.

WRITTEN BY
ANDRIA AND
CINDY GILLELAND

Across the wall, from left to right:

CIVIL WAR   WORLD WAR I   WORLD WAR II   KOREA   VIETNAM

The wall contains eleven sections, eight of which bear the names of Dawson County veterans. Beneath the center inscription are crossed flags and an eagle.

Three of the sections contain the names of Confederate veterans, 288 in all. One section contains names of veterans of World War I, three World War II, one Korea; and one Vietnam.

Decatur County, Bainbridge

LOCATION: Willis Park, facing North Broad Street	**DATE:** 1906 (McKenney)
STYLE: Statue of a soldier on a cylindrical column	**BUILDER:** UDC and the city of Bainbridge

C.S.A.

TO OUR CONFEDERATE SOLDIERS
1861–1865.

ERECTED BY THE BAINBRIDGE CHAPTER
OF UNITED DAUGHTERS OF THE CONFEDERACY
AND THE CITY OF BAINBRIDGE.
1905.

A bronze tablet at the base of the monument reads:

THE BAINBRIDGE VOLUNTEERS
LATER
THE BAINBRIDGE INDEPENDENTS
ORGANIZED 1859, BY
CAPTAIN CHARLES G. CAMPBELL,
ASSEMBLED HERE IN MARCH 1861 AND
ENTERED SERVICE UNDER THE COMMAND
OF CAPTAIN JOHN W. EVANS AS
COMPANY G, 1ST GEORGIA REGIMENT
W.P.A. 1936 U.D.C.

Willis Park was once known as Monument Square. It is the site of the old courthouse. The monument was dedicated April 26, 1906. Linda Gordon, niece of Gen. John B. Gordon, unveiled the monument (McKenney).

A battle flag is carved on the front of the column. The top of the column is decorated with carvings of cannon barrels, rifles, sabers, and anchors.

The soldier is standing at rest.

DeKalb County, Decatur

LOCATION: South side of the old courthouse, East Court Square | **DATE:** 1908

STYLE: Obelisk | **BUILDER:** The men, women, and children of DeKalb County

FABRICATOR: Butler Granite Co. of Marietta (McKenney)

ERECTED 1908

ERECTED
BY THE MEN AND WOMEN AND
CHILDREN OF DEKALB COUNTY,
TO THE MEMORY OF THE
SOLDIERS AND SAILORS
OF THE CONFEDERACY,
OF WHOSE VIRTUES IN PEACE
AND IN WAR WE ARE WITNESSES,
TO THE END THAT JUSTICE
MAY BE DONE AND THAT THE
TRUTH PERISH NOT.

1861–1865

AFTER FORTY TWO YEARS
ANOTHER GENERATION BEARS
WITNESS TO THE FUTURE
THAT THESE MEN WERE OF A
COVENANT KEEPING RACE WHO
HELD FAST TO THE FAITH AS IT WAS
GIVEN BY THE FATHERS OF THE
REPUBLIC.

MODEST IN PROSPERITY,
GENTLE IN PEACE, BRAVE IN BATTLE
AND UNDESPAIRING IN DEFEAT,
THEY KNEW NO LAW OF LIFE BUT
LOYALTY AND TRUTH AND CIVIC
FAITH, AND TO THESE VIRTUES THEY
CONSECRATED THEIR STRENGTH.

C.S.A

THESE MEN HELD THAT THE
STATES MADE THE UNION,
THAT THE CONSTITUTION IS THE
EVIDENCE OF THE COVENANT,
THAT THE PEOPLE OF THE STATE
ARE SUBJECT TO NO POWER
EXCEPT AS THEY HAVE AGREED
THAT FREE CONVENTION BINDS
THE PARTIES TO IT, THAT THERE
IS SANCTITY IN OATHS AND
OBLIGATION IN CONTRACTS,
AND IN DEFENSE OF THESE
PRINCIPLES
THEY MUTUALLY PLEDGED THEIR
LIVES
THEIR FORTUNES AND THEIR
SACRED HONOR.

1861–1865

HOW WELL THEY KEPT THE
FAITH IS FAINTLY WRITTEN
IN THE RECORDS OF THE ARMIES
AND THE HISTORY OF THE TIMES.
WE WHO KNEW THEM TESTIFY THAT
AS THEIR COURAGE WAS WITHOUT
A PRECEDENT THEIR FORTITUDE
HAS BEEN WITHOUT A PARALLEL,
MAY THEIR PROSPERITY BE WORTHY.

C.S.A.

The monument was dedicated on April 27, 1908. The cost was $2,000. The dedication had been scheduled for the previous November but the shaft fell and was shattered. The emphatic constitutional argument was written by Hooper Alexander, who spoke at the dedication (McKenney). Alexander was a lawyer, state legislator, and US Attorney. He spoke also at the dedication of the Hall County monument in Gainesville.

The decorations include the drape over the obelisk, tassels hanging from the drape, four shells at the top of the plinth, and a flag of uncertain design. The long inscriptions cover all four sides of the plinth.

DeKalb County, Decatur

	LOCATION: Decatur Cemetery, Church Street	
DATE: 1984	STYLE: Granite cross	BUILDER: UDC

HONORING THE
MEMORY OF
THOSE WHO FELL
AND SERVED
IN THE SERVICE OF THE
CONFEDERATE STATES OF
AMERICA 1861–1865

ERECTED BY THE
AGNES LEE
CHAPTER
U.D.C.
DECATUR, GA.
1984

DeKalb County, Stone Mountain

The carving on the face of Stone Mountain is the largest and most famous Confederate memorial in existence. The project was conceived in 1914 by Caroline Helen Jemison Plane, president of the Atlanta Chapter of the UDC. Work began under the direction of Gutzon Borglum in 1923. After delays brought on by financial problems, artistic disputes, depression and war, the state of Georgia took on the project in 1958 and completed the monument with its new design: Lee, Davis, and Jackson on horseback. The monument was dedicated in 1970.

DeKalb County, Stone Mountain

LOCATION: Stone Mountain City Cemetery	DATE: 2007	STYLE: Obelisk
BUILDERS: SCV and other organizations named on the monument		

DEDICATED TO
THE MORE THAN 225 UNKNOWN
SOLDIERS AND VETERANS
BURIED WITHIN THE
STONE MOUNTAIN CITY CEMETERY
WHO SERVED HONORABLY IN THE
SERVICE OF THE
CONFEDERATE STATES OF AMERICA
1861–1865

APRIL 26, 2007

ERECTED BY THE
SONS OF CONFEDERATE VETERANS
CONFEDERATE MEMORIAL CAMP No. 1432

WITH THE SUPPORT FROM THE FOLLOWING
ORGANIZATIONS:

THE OLD GUARD OF THE GATE CITY GUARD
GEN. JOHN B. GORDON CAMP No. 46 S.C.V.
PYTHAGORAS LODGE No. 41, FREE AND ACCEPTED MASONS
DEKALB CHAPTER No. 85, ROYAL ARCH MASONS
DEKALB COUNCIL No. 57, ROYAL AND SELECT MASTERS
DEKALB COMMANDRY No. 38, KNIGHTS TEMPLAR

GEORGIA'S CONFEDERATE MONUMENTS

Dodge County, Eastman

LOCATION: Courthouse grounds, Courthouse Circle	**DATE:** 1910
STYLE: Statue of a soldier on a column	**BUILDER:** UDC
FABRICATOR: McNeel Marble Co. (McNeel Memorials)	

ERECTED BY THE
FANNIE GORDON CHAPTER
UNITED DAUGHTERS
OF THE CONFEDERACY
APRIL 1910.

(Fannie Gordon was wife of John B. Gordon.)

"NO NATION ROSE SO PURE
AND WHITE;
NONE EVER FELL SO SPOTLESS."

(This is an odd misquote of "The Grand Old Bard" by Philip Stanhope Worsley.)

TO OUR CONFEDERATE
SOLDIERS
1861–1865

"THE PRINCIPLES FOR WHICH
THEY FOUGHT CAN NEVER DIE."

CONFEDERATE
DEAD

"TO THOSE WHO FOUGHT
AND LIVED,
TO THOSE WHO FOUGHT
AND DIED."

THIS STONE IS ERECTED
TO KEEP FRESH IN MEMORY
THE NOBLE DEEDS OF
THESE DEVOTED SONS.

NO BRAVER SOLDIERS,
NO TRUER PATRIOTS EVER
ADORNED THE HISTORY OF
ANY NATION, THEY HAVE
WON THEIR TITLE TO AN
IMMORTALITY OF LOVE
AND REVERENCE.

"NOR SHALL YOUR GLORY
BE FORGOT,
WHILE FAME HER RECORD
KEEPS."

(From "The Bivouac of the Dead" by Theodore O'Hara)

On the front are a rifle and a saber crossed with a flagstaff, all draped with the flag. The soldier is standing at rest.

The cost of the monument was either $2,000 or $3,000. The monument was originally located on a downtown street. The height is 30 feet (McKenney).

Dooly County, Vienna

LOCATION: Park in front of the courthouse, facing Third Street	DATE: 1908 (McKenney)
STYLE: Statue of a soldier on a pedestal	BUILDER: UDC

CONFEDERATE

DOOLY COUNTY
ERECTS THIS MEMORIAL TO
HER CONFEDERATE SOLDIERS
1861–1865

The front of the monument contains an unusual image: outside a tent are three stacked rifles from which hang a canteen and a cartridge box. There are impressions in the stone that seem to represent footprints walking into the tent.
The monument was built at a cost of $2,000 and dedicated November 26, 1908 (McKenney).

On the rear are a CSA monogram inside a wreath; crossed battle flags; and the Southern Cross of Honor. The soldier is standing at rest.

Dougherty County, Albany

LOCATION: Confederate Memorial Park on Philema Road. This site, the fourth for the Dougherty monument, is actually in Lee County, just north of the county line.

DATE: 1901 (CSMA, p. 86)	STYLE: Statue of a soldier on a pedestal	BUILDER: LMA

OUR CONFEDERATE
DEAD.
1861–1865.

THEY FOUGHT NOT FOR CON-
QUEST, BUT FOR LIBERTY AND
THEIR OWN HOMES.

THIS MONUMENT IS ERECTED
UNDER AUSPICES OF THE LADIES'
MEMORIAL ASSOCIATION OF DOUGH-
ERTY COUNTY, GEORGIA, TO THE
MEN
WHO FOUGHT IN THE CONFEDERATE
ARMY IN DEFENSE OF CONSTITU-
TIONAL LIBERTY.

THESE MEN NEED NO EULOGY,
FOR "THEIR WORKS DO FOLLOW
THEM."

(From Revelation 14:13, King James Version: "And I heard a voice from heaven saying unto me, Write, Blessed are the dead which die in the Lord from henceforth: Yea, saith the Spirit, that they may rest from their labours; and their works do follow them.")

When the monument was in the cemetery, there was a stone marker nearby:

IN MEMORY OF
THESE SEVEN
UNKNOWN
CONFEDERATE
SOLDIERS
WHO DIED IN WAR
BETWEEN THE STATES
1860 1865 [SIC]
ERECTED BY
DOUGHERTY COUNTY
CHAPTER U.D.C.
MILDRED RUTHERFORD
CHAPTER CHILDREN
OF CONFEDERACY
1952

This marker remains in the cemetery at graves of the unknown dead.

Also remaining is the concrete pad on which the monument rested.

This monument contains little decoration, only two stars on each of the four sides, above the inscriptions.

The monument's cost was approximately $1,500. It was unveiled at its original location (Pine Avenue and Jackson Street) on November 13, 1901. After being hit by car in 1930s, it was moved to park near the old auditorium. At some point it was put in Riverside Cemetery (McKenney). In 2000 Confederate Memorial Park was opened on Philema Road, north of Albany in Lee County, as a site for the monument. The soldier is standing at rest.

Douglas County, Douglasville

LOCATION: Courthouse grounds, Hospital Drive and Dorris Road		**DATE:** 1914
STYLE: Statue of a soldier on a column	**BUILDER:** UDC	
FABRICATOR: McNeel Marble Co. (McNeel Memorials)		

DOUGLAS
COUNTY
HEROES

ERECTED BY
DOUGLASVILLE CHAPTER
UNITED DAUGHTERS
OF THE CONFEDERACY.
1914.

The monument was moved to its current location at the new courthouse in 1998 (UDC 2002). The old courthouse is still standing and is used for other purposes.

"CSA" is carved on two sides of the column. On the front of the plinth are the dates of the war inside crossed sabers.

The soldier is standing at rest.

GEORGIA'S CONFEDERATE MONUMENTS

Early County, Blakely

LOCATION: Courthouse grounds, Court Square		DATE: 1909	STYLE: Obelisk
BUILDER: UDC	FABRICATOR: McNeel Marble Co. (McNeel Memorials)		

CONFEDERATE DEAD

"A TRIBUTE OF LOVE,
TO THE NOBLE
CONFEDERATE SOLDIERS
WHO CHEERFULLY
OFFERED THEIR LIVES
IN DEFENSE OF THE
RIGHT OF LOCAL
SELF-GOVERNMENT,
AND TO THOSE WHO
FOUGHT AND SURVIVED."

ERECTED BY
THE BLAKELY
CHAPTER
U.D.C. 1909.

"LEST WE FORGET."

On the front of the plinth are a flag, partly furled around its staff, and the dates of the war. Another panel shows crossed sabers.

Next to monument is a flag pole which, according to the tablet at its base, is the "last original Confederate flag staff still standing in Georgia." The tablet, erected by the Georgia Historical Commission in 1954, says that the pole of long leaf pine was erected in May 1861.

The monument was dedicated on Confederate Memorial Day, 1909. It is still in its original location. The cost was $2,000 (McKenney).

Effingham County, Springfield

LOCATION: Courthouse grounds, North Laurel Street	DATE: 1923	STYLE: Obelisk
BUILDER: UDC	FABRICATOR: McNeel Marble Co. (McNeel Memorials)	

TO HONOR THE
CONFEDERATE HEROES
OF
EFFINGHAM COUNTY

CONFEDERATE

ERECTED BY
SALZBURGER CHAPTER
UNITED DAUGHTERS OF
THE CONFEDERACY
APRIL 26, 1923

On the stone below the plinth, "C.S.A." is set inside a wreath, with "1861" and "1865" flanking the wreath.

McKenney names Capitol Monument Company of Statesboro as the fabricator, but the monument is included on the list of McNeel's projects compiled by the company.

The obelisk and the base are made of marble.

Effingham County, Springfield

LOCATION: Veterans Park of Effingham County, Georgia Highway 21 and West First Street Extension		
DATE: 2003	**STYLE:** Memorial wall	**BUILDER:** A committee of local citizens
DESIGNER: Monica Mastrianni of Bazemore, Mastrianni, Wilson		

    The wall contains tablets listing the men of Effingham County who served in all wars from the Revolutionary War to Afghanistan and Iraq. There are nearly 750 names for the Civil War.

    The committee raised funds from private sources. Much of the work was performed with volunteer labor. No public funds were used. Information concerning the date, builder, designer, and source of funds was obtained from the Veterans Park of Effingham County website (www.effinghamveteranspark.com).

Effingham County, Guyton

LOCATION: Ferguson Cemetery, Cemetery Street | **STYLE:** Small stone column and gateway.

On the lintel:

CONFEDERATE DEAD
REMEMBERED

On the shaft:

TO THE UNKNOWN
CONFEDERATE DEAD.

On a gravestone near the marker:

IN THIS PLOT
ARE BURIED
TWENTY SIX
UNKNOWN
CONFEDERATE
SOLDIERS
DIED IN
GEN HOSP
GUYTON GA
1864–65

Elbert County, Elberton

LOCATION: Sutton Square, facing South McIntosh Street	**DATE**: 1898

STYLE: Statue of a soldier on column

BUILDERS: The Memorial Association and UDC (McKenney)

ELBERT COUNTY
TO HER
CONFEDERATE DEAD

CORNER STONE LAID BY
GRAND LODGE OF GA.
F. & A. M.
JULY 16, 1898
JOHN H. JONES, A.G.M.

LET THE STRANGER, WHO IN FUTURE TIMES READS
THIS INSCRIPTION, RECOGNIZE THAT THESE WERE
MEN, WHOM POWER COULD NOT CORRUPT, WHOM
DEATH COULD NOT TERRIFY, WHOM DEFEAT COULD NOT DISHONOR.
LET THE GEORGIAN OF ANOTHER GENERATION
REMEMBER, THAT THE STATE TAUGHT THEM HOW
TO LIVE, AND HOW TO DIE, AND THAT FROM HER
BROKEN FORTUNES, SHE HAS PRESERVED FOR HER
CHILDREN, THE PRICELESS TREASURES OF THEIR MEMORIES

*(This is a variation of a passage from a speech by William Henry Trescot.
See the text for the Cartersville monument in Bartow County.)*

THIS MONUMENT PERPETUATES
THE MEMORY OF
THOSE WHO, TRUE TO THE INSTINCT
OF THEIR BIRTH
FAITHFUL TO THE TEACHINGS
OF THEIR FATHERS
CONSTANT IN THEIR LOVE FOR
THE SOUTH, DIED IN
THE PERFORMANCE OF THEIR DUTY.

THESE MEN HAVE GLORIFIED
A FALLEN CAUSE
BY THE SIMPLE MANHOOD
OF THEIR LIVES, THE
PATIENT ENDURANCE
OF SUFFERING, AND THE
HEROISM OF DEATH, AND WHO
IN THE DARK
HOURS OF IMPRISONMENT,
IN THE HOPELESSNESS
OF THE HOSPITAL, FOUND SUPPORT
AND CONSOLATION
IN THE BELIEF, THAT AT HOME
THEY WOULD NOT BE
FORGOTTEN.

WITH TRUE SOUTHERN DEVOTION
MRS. R.M. HEARD,
AND HER CO-LABORERS,
HAVE ERECTED THIS,
MONUMENT.

The monument was dedicated on July 15, 1898. The cost was $1,500. The original 7-foot statue of the soldier was "instantly unpopular." The soldier was overweight and was shod in "clodhopper boots." The statue was vandalized in August 1900 and buried in the square. The present statue was erected at some later date. "Dutchy," as the unpopular statue was known, was disinterred in 1982 and put in the Elberton Granite Museum (McKenney).

A battle flag is carved on the front of the plinth. The staff is unbroken but the flag is tattered. Above the flag are the dates of the war. A triangular arrangement of cannonballs appears on a band above the plinth, front and rear. On the adjacent side, this band displays crossed sabers and crossed cannon barrels.

The sculptor of the statue now on the column was Arthur Beter (Wiggins).

The soldier is standing at rest.

Elbert County, Elberton

LOCATION: Elbert County Memorial Park, Hartwell Highway, north of downtown		
DATE: Ca. 1992 (Anne Jenson)	**STYLE:** Memorial wall	**BUILDER:** William Arnold Edwards
FABRICATORS: Southern Granite Co. and Anne Jenson Etching Co.		

ELBERT COUNTY'S DEAD IN THE CIVIL WAR

IN CHARACTERS OF LIVING LIGHT
THAT TELL A WONDROUS STORY,
THEIR DEEDS HAVE BRIGHTENED MANY A PAGE
WITH NEVER-DYING GLORY.

This memorial wall is one of several in the park honoring the county's dead in all wars. The memorial park was established in 1923. William Edwards was the retired founder of the Southern Granite Co. The Anne Jenson Etching Co. did the lettering.

The polished center of the granite wall contains a Confederate Battle Flag, images of Jefferson Davis and Robert E. Lee (with Traveller), and scenes of camp and battle. On the sides are 283 names.

The information on the builder and fabricators was provided by Carolyn Miller of the Lexington Blue Granite Company. The approximate date was provided by Anne Jenson (conversations and correspondence, July 2012). The Miller family and their company (then the Service Granite Company) were instrumental in the creation of the park and its various memorials.

Emanuel County, Swainsboro

LOCATION: Park in center of town, West Main Street	**DATE:** 1979
STYLE: Bronze tablet	**BUILDER:** UDC and Emanuel Historic Preservation Society

IN MEMORY OF
EMANUEL COUNTY'S CIVIL WAR SOLDIERS
1861–1865

EMANUEL RANGERS   BEN HILL GUARDS
ROUGH AND READY GUARDS   BROWN GUARDS
McLEOD VOLUNTEERS

PRESENTED BY THE EMANUEL RANGERS CHAPTER,
UNITED DAUGHTERS OF THE CONFEDERACY
& THE EMANUEL HISTORIC PRESERVATION SOCIETY.
1979

The tablet originally hung inside the Emanuel County Courthouse. When a new courthouse was built in 2002, a park was put on the site of the old structure. The tablet now hangs on a brick column at one of the park entrances.

Fayette County, Fayetteville

LOCATION: Courthouse grounds, facing Lee Street and East Lanier Avenue		
DATE: 1934	STYLE: Memorial stone with a bronze tablet	BUILDER: UDC

IN MEMORY OF THE
CONFEDERATE HEROES
OF
FAYETTE COUNTY
1861–1865

ERECTED BY
FAYETTE COUNTY CHAPTER
U. D. C.
1934

This monument, built during a time of great economic hardship, was one of the last built before a renewed interest developed more than 50 years later.

The stone is granite.

Floyd County, Rome

LOCATION: At the summit of Myrtle Hill Cemetery | DATE: 1887 (CSMA, p. 153)

BUILDERS: The women of Rome

FABRICATOR: The statue was made by the McNeel Marble Co. (McKenney)

STYLE: Statue of a soldier on a pedestal

ERECTED BY THE WOMEN OF ROME
TO THE MEMORY OF
THE SOLDIERS OF FLOYD
COUNTY. GEORGIA.
WHO DIED IN DEFENCE OF
THE CONFEDERATE STATES
OF AMERICA.
1861–1865.

THEY HAVE CROSSED THE RIVER
AND SLEEP BENEATH THE SHADE.

THIS MONUMENT
IS THE TESTIMONY OF THE PRESENT
TO THE FUTURE THAT THESE WERE
THEY WHO KEPT THE FAITH AS IT WAS
GIVEN THEM BY THE FATHERS.
BE IT KNOWN BY THIS TOKEN
THAT THESE MEN WERE TRUE TO
THE TRADITIONS OF THEIR LINEAGE;
BOLD, GENEROUS AND FREE;
FIRM IN CONVICTION OF THE RIGHT;
READY AT THEIR COUNTRY'S CALL;
STEADFAST IN THEIR DUTY;
FAITHFUL EVEN IN DESPAIR;
AND ILLUSTRATED
IN THE UNFLINCHING HEROISM
OF THEIR DEATHS
THE FREE BORN COURAGE
OF THEIR LIVES.

HOW WELL
THEY SERVED THEIR FAITH
THEIR PEOPLE KNOW;
A THOUSAND BATTLEFIELDS ATTEST;
DUNGEON AND HOSPITAL BEAR
WITNESS.
TO THEIR SONS THEY LEFT

BUT HONOR AND THEIR COUNTRY.
LET THIS STONE FOREVER WARN
THOSE WHO KEEP THESE VALLEYS
THAT ONLY THEIR SIRES ARE DEAD:
THE PRINCIPLES FOR WHICH THEY
FOUGHT CAN NEVER DIE.

At the foot of the column is a bronze tablet:

MYRTLE HILL CEMETERY

ESTABLISHED AS THE SECOND CITY
CEMETERY IN 1857. NEARBY ON
THIS PEAK LIE BURIED COLONEL
ZACHARIAH B. HARGROVE AND
COLONEL DANIEL R. MITCHELL,
TWO OF THE CITY'S FOUNDERS.

ON THE AXSON FAMILY LOT IS
BURIED ELLEN LOU AXSON, THE
FIRST WIFE OF FORMER PRESIDENT
WOODROW WILSON.

LOCATED IN THE CEMETERY ARE
HANDSOME MONUMENTS
COMMEMORATING
GENERAL NATHAN B. FORREST,
THE WOMEN OF THE CONFEDERACY,
FLOYD COUNTY'S CONFEDERATE
WAR DEAD, AND CHARLES W.
GRAVES AS REPRESENTATIVE OF
THE KNOWN DEAD OF WORLD WAR I.

THIS TABLET PLACED BY
THE ROME AREA HERITAGE
FOUNDATION
1975

The monument was unveiled on Confederate Memorial Day, 1887. The pedestal was topped originally with a large urn. There were four smaller urns at the base of the column. The large urn was replaced by the soldier in 1909.

The monument was rededicated on Confederate Memorial Day of that year. The original cost was $1,000 (McKenney).

The Great Seal of the Confederacy is engraved on the front face of the column. On the rear is a CSA monogram encircled by a wreath. The soldier is standing at rest.

Floyd County, Rome

LOCATION: The foot of Myrtle Hill Cemetery, South Broad Street and Branham Avenue

| **DATE:** 1910 | **STYLE:** Obelisk with two pairs of statues | **BUILDER:** SCV (Knight, p. 242) |

FABRICATOR: Georgia Granite and Marble Co. (McKenney)

SCULPTOR: J. Wolz (Knight, p. 241)

1861–1865

TO THE WOMEN OF THE CONFEDERACY.

SHE WAS OBEDIENT
TO THE GOD SHE ADORED
AND TRUE TO EVERY VOW
SHE MADE TO MAN.
SHE WAS LOYAL TO THE COUNTRY SHE
LOVED SO WELL
AND UPON ITS ALTAR LAID HUSBAND,
SIRE AND SON.
THE HOME SHE LOVED TO SERVE WAS
GRACED
WITH SINCERITY OF LIFE AND DEVOTION
OF HEART.
SHE REARED HER SONS TO UNSELFISH
CHIVALRY
AND HER DAUGHTERS
TO SPOTLESS PURITY.
HER CHILDREN DELIGHT
TO GIVE HER HONOR
AND LOVE TO SPEAK HER PRAISE.

ERECTED
MARCH 9TH 1910.

1861–1865

TO THE WOMEN OF THE CONFEDERACY.

WHOSE PURITY, WHOSE FIDELITY,
WHOSE COURAGE,
WHOSE GENTLE GENIUS
IN LOVE AND COUNSEL
KEPT THE HOME SECURE,
THE FAMILY A SCHOOL
OF VIRTUE, THE STATE
A COURT OF HONOR;
WHO MADE OF WAR A SEASON
OF HEROISM AND OF
PEACE A TIME OF HEALING;
THE GUARDIANS OF
OUR TRANQUILITY AND
OF OUR STRENGTH.

WOODROW WILSON

The style of this monument is similar to the women's monument in Macon: two sets of statues on opposite sides of the shaft, one pair depicting a young woman with a child at her knee, and on the opposite side of the obelisk the same woman aiding a wounded soldier. Beneath the statue of woman and child are the anxious words "NEWS FROM THE FRONT." The words under the statue of woman and wounded soldier read "AN ANGEL OF MERCY."

In 1952 this statue, along with the adjacent Forrest monument, was moved from downtown Rome to Myrtle Hill Cemetery (McKenney). The author possesses post cards showing both monuments in their original locations. The monument was built before Woodrow Wilson's presidency. In 1910 he was president of Princeton University. His first wife, Ellen Axson Wilson, grew up in Rome, where her father was a Presbyterian minister, as was Wilson's father.

The shaft is made of Georgia marble. The cost of the monument was $4,500. The unattributed inscription was written by the Reverend G. A. Nunnally, former president of Mercer University. The monument was originally located at the intersection of Broad and Third (Knight, 1:241–43).

Floyd County, Rome

LOCATION: The foot of Myrtle Hill Cemetery, South Broad Street and Branham Avenue

DATE: 1906	STYLE: Statue of General Nathan Bedford Forrest on a column	BUILDER: UDC

ERECTED
BY
N. B. FORREST CHAPTER
UNITED DAUGHTERS OF THE
CONFEDERACY
MAY 3RD
1906.

N. B. FORREST

"HE POSSESSED THAT RARE TACT,
UNLEARNABLE FROM BOOKS,
WHICH ENABLED HIM, NOT ONLY
EFFECTUALLY, TO CONTROL HIS
MEN, BUT TO ATTACH THEM TO HIM,
PERSONALLY, "WITH HOOKS OF
STEEL."
WOLSELEY.

*(British Field Marshall Garnet Joseph Wolseley,
First Viscount Wolseley, traveled to the
Confederacy as a young officer
to observe the war.)*

ON SUNDAY, MAY 3RD, 1863,
GEN. NATHAN BEDFORD FORREST,
BY HIS INDOMITABLE WILL,
AFTER A RUNNING FIGHT OF THREE
DAYS AND NIGHTS, WITH 410 MEN,
CAPTURED COL. A. D. STREIGHT'S
RAIDERS, NUMBERING 1600,
THEREBY
SAVING ROME FROM DESTRUCTION.

"FORREST'S CAPACITY FOR WAR
SEEMED ONLY TO BE LIMITED BY THE
OPPORTUNITIES FOR IT'S DISPLAY."
GEN. BEAUREGARD.

"HIS CAVALRY WILL TRAVEL
A HUNDRED MILES IN LESS
TIME THAN OURS WILL TEN."
GEN. W. T. SHERMAN.

Pediments on the front and rear above the plinth contain the date 1861. The adjacent pediments on the sides show the date 1865.

The statue is in a small park next to the monument to the women of the Confederacy. (See previous entry for information concerning the relocation of both monuments.)

On the rear are crossed sabers and a bugle. "CSA" is inscribed on each of the four pediments beneath the statue. Stars surround the column below these pediments.

A battle flag with a broken staff is on the front of the column.

Forsyth County, Cumming

LOCATION: Veterans Memorial Boulevard, south of downtown Cumming		**DATE:** 1992
STYLE: Memorial stone topped with bronze artifacts		**BUILDER:** City of Cumming
SCULPTOR: Gregory Johnson (www.gregoryjohnson.biz and brochure on City of Cumming's website, www.cityofcumming.net, both accessed July 2012)		

VETERAN'S WAR MEMORIAL

DEDICATED IN THE YEAR OF OUR LORD 1992
PROJECT COMMISSIONED BY
THE CITY OF CUMMING

REALIZING ANEW, THE FULL PORTION
OF SACRIFICE PAID BY THE SONS AND
DAUGHTERS OF CUMMING AND FORSYTH
COUNTY, GEORGIA, IN THE DEFENSE
OF LIFE AND INDIVIDUAL RIGHTS,
WE THE CITIZENS, IN GRATITUDE
AND HONOR, DEDICATE THIS MONUMENT
TO THEIR MEMORY.
AND IN DOING SO, PLEDGE TO
PRESERVE AND PROTECT THE FREEDOMS
FOR WHICH THEY SO BRAVELY FOUGHT.
THIS PLACE WILL BE HELD IN
REVERENCE FOR ALL THOSE WHO WISH
TO PAUSE AND REMEMBER HOW WE CAME
TO LIVE IN THIS SWEET LAND OF
LIBERTY.

AMERICA, AMERICA,
GOD SHED HIS GRACE ON THEE.

The monument consists of marble blocks, one for the veterans of each war. Each element is topped with bronze artifacts. The Civil War component contains the inscription "CIVIL WAR 1861–1865" and the names of 110 Confederate soldiers from the county. On top are a canteen, a kepi, a bugle, and a small bird.

The Confederate memorial is one element in a large monument to the veterans of all American wars. The inscription appears on the stone in front of the monument.

GEORGIA'S CONFEDERATE MONUMENTS

Franklin County, Carnesville

LOCATION: Courthouse grounds, Athens Street	**DATE:** 1910
STYLE: Statue of a soldier on a column	**BUILDER:** UDC
FABRICATOR: McNeel Marble Co. (McNeel Memorials)	

TO OUR
CONFEDERATE
SOLDIERS

IN MEMORY OF
THE
FRANKLIN COUNTY
VETERANS
FROM THE
MILLICAN CHAPTER
U. D. C.
AUG. 10, 1910

"THIS, WE RAISE
A LOVING TRIBUTE,
TO THE PAST, PRESENT
AND FUTURE."

"CSA" is engraved below the soldier's rear, on the side of the column facing away from the courthouse. Lower on this same side are the dates of the war and a battle flag crossed with another flag of uncertain design.

The soldier is marching with his rifle on his shoulder, a rare form for Georgia's Confederate monuments.

The monument is set very close to the building, and the soldier faces the courthouse.

According to McKenney, the widow of General Longstreet was present at the dedication. Both McKenney (1993) and Wiggins (2006) state that the rifle was missing and the cannonballs were damaged. Since 2006 the rifle has been replaced and the cannonballs repaired.

The final quote shown above is also found on the Polk County monument. The author has not been able to identify the source.

Fulton County, Atlanta

LOCATION: Oakland Cemetery, Oakland Avenue	DATE: 1874 (CSMA, p. 95)
STYLE: Obelisk	BUILDER: LMA

OUR
CONFEDERATE
DEAD
1873

ERECTED BY
THE ATLANTA LADIES MEMORIAL ASSOCIATION

This 65-foot-high obelisk stands on one of the main avenues in the cemetery, near the section with row upon row of Confederate graves.

The Atlanta Ladies' Memorial Association began raising funds for the project in 1869. The cornerstone was laid on October 15, 1870, the day of Lee's funeral. The ladies continued raising money and the shaft was erected in January 1874. The monument was dedicated April 26 of that year. The cost was $8,000, a low amount made possible by the donation of the granite by the Stone Mountain Granite Company and free transportation by the Georgia Railroad (CSMA, p. 91ff).

Fulton County, Atlanta

LOCATION: Oakland Cemetery, Oakland Avenue	**DATE:** 1895 (CSMA, pp. 100–102)
STYLE: Statue of a lion modeled after the Lion of Lucerne	
BUILDER: LMA	**SCULPTOR:** T. M. Brady

UNKNOWN CONFEDERATE DEAD

T. M. BRADY Sc.
CANTON GA.

ERECTED BY
THE ATLANTA LADIES MEMORIAL ASSOCIATION 1894

The Lion of Atlanta is located in the section of Oakland Cemetery containing the graves of unknown Confederate soldiers.

The lion was unveiled in April 1895, not the date carved on the statue. It weighs 30,000 pounds. At the time of the dedication, 3,000 unknown Confederate dead were reinterred (McKenney).

The lion and the base are made of marble from Tate, Georgia (UDC 2002).

The lion's head rests on a Confederate Battle Flag.

Fulton County, Atlanta

| LOCATION: Oakland Cemetery, Oakland Avenue | STYLE: Stone pillars |

ERECTED BY
THE ATLANTA LADIES MEMORIAL ASSOCIATION
1892

There are two identical pillars in the Confederate section, one near the eastern end and one near the western end.

Fulton County, Atlanta

LOCATION: Oakland Cemetery, Oakland Avenue	**STYLE**: Memorial stone with a bronze tablet

ERECTED IN MEMORY OF OUR CONFEDERATE SOLDIERS
BY THE
ATLANTA LADIES MEMORIAL ASSOCIATION
MRS. WM. M. RAPP...PRESIDENT
MRS. R.B. BLACKBURN .. V. PRES. MRS. A.F. BLACK .. SECT.
MRS. J.A. BEALL .. TREAS.   MRS. H.H. ELLIS .. COR. SECT.
MRS. E.B. WILLIAMS ... CHAIRMAN OF MARKING GRAVES
"LEST WE FORGET"
DEDICATED APRIL 26, 1950

Fulton County, Atlanta

LOCATION: Westview Cemetery, Westview Drive	**DATE**: 1889 (Rodgers, p. 17)
STYLE: Statue of a soldier on a column	
BUILDER: Confederate Veterans Association of Fulton County	

ERECTED
BY THE
CONFEDERATE
VETERANS'
ASSOCIATION
OF
FULTON CO. GA.
IN MEMORY OF
OUR DEAD COMRADES

One side of the pedestal contains carvings of crossed sabers and a plow with the inscription:

"THEY SHALL BEAT THEIR SWORDS
INTO PLOUGH SHARES."

On the other side of the pedestal are crossed rifles with bayonets. In the space between the rifles is a pruning hook. The Old Testament quote is continued:

"AND THEIR SPEARS
INTO PRUNING HOOKS."

On a lower part of the base, the quote continues:

"NATION SHALL NOT LIFT UP
SWORD AGAINST NATION."

And on the opposite side it is completed:

"NEITHER SHALL THEY LEARN
WAR ANY MORE."

("They shall beat their swords into ploughshares, and their spears into pruning hooks: nation shall not lift sword against nation, neither shall they learn war any more." [Isaiah 2:4 and Micah 4:3, King James Version].)

On another surface are carved a battlefield grave, a mound of dirt with a cross, a flag, and battlefield debris.

"OF LIBERTY BORN OF A PATRIOT'S
DREAM
OF A STORM-CRADLED NATION THAT
FELL."

(From "Lines on a Confederate Note" by Major Sidney Alroy Jonas)

The complete stanza of the Jonas poem reads: "Show it to those who will lend an ear / To the tale that this paper can tell / Of Liberty born of the patriot's dream, / Of a storm-cradled nation that fell." (In some versions "trifle" is in the place of "paper.")

Vertical cannon barrels, muzzles down, form pilasters at the corners of the plinth. Just beneath the statue are more cannons, pointing outward, with piles of cannon balls in between.

The statue was carved in Cararra, Italy (CVA p. 17). The soldier is standing at rest.

GEORGIA'S CONFEDERATE MONUMENTS

Fulton County, Atlanta

LOCATION: State Capitol, Washington Street	
DATE: 1907 (georgiainfo.Galileo.usg.edu, accessed June 2009)	**STYLE:** Equestrian statue
BUILDER: State of Georgia (according to Buzzett, the Gordon Memorial Commission)	
SCULPTOR: Solon H. Borglum (georgiainfo.Galileo.usg.edu, accessed June 2009)	

GORDON

SPOTTSYLVANIA C H

TWELFTH OF MAY 1864

"GENERAL LEE TO THE REAR"

The statue portrays the general as a man of middle age, when he commanded the United Confederate Veterans, not the youthful general who rose to prominence late in the war.

According to McNeel Memorials, the base of this monument was the work of the McNeel Marble Company.

On the right side of the base, a bronze tablet displays in bas relief the "Lee to the Rear" episode that occurred at Spotsylvania. Gordon is shown on horseback, blocking Lee and Traveller and preventing Lee from leading the counterattack on May 12.

On the opposite side of the base another bronze tablet shows Gordon the postwar statesman, standing erect between two seated female figures, one representing Georgia and the other the United States. Beneath Gordon are the words "GOVERNOR," "PATRIOT," and "SENATOR."

The tablet on the rear of the monument summarizes Gordon's military, business, and political career.

Fulton County, Atlanta

LOCATION: Piedmont Park at the 14th Street entrance	**DATE:** 1911

STYLE: Bronze statues of a soldier and an angel on a stone pedestal

SCULPTOR: Allen G. Newman

CEASE FIRING—PEACE IS PROCLAIMED

IN BELLO PACEQUE PRIMUS

The words "CEASE FIRING—PEACE IS PROCLAIMED" appear below the statues, as the exhausted and relieved soldier looks up toward the angel of peace.

Below the angel's welcomed words is the emblem of the Old Guard of the Gate City Guard, which contains the Latin sentence: "IN BELLO PACEQUE PRIMUS."

A long inscription on the bronze tablet on the front tells the story of the Gate City Guard's "Mission of Peace" in 1897 and the dedication of the monument in 1911.

CEASE FIRING—PEACE IS PROCLAIMED

RESURGENS
1847 ATLANTA, GA. 1865

IN MEMORY
OF
FATHER THOMAS O'REILLY
WHO IN NOVEMBER 1864 BY HIS
COURAGEOUS PROTEST TO THE FEDERAL
FORCES PREPARING TO BURN AND
EVACUATE THE CITY SAVED FROM THE
CONFLAGRATION THE FOLLOWING
BUILDINGS THEN LOCATED IN THIS
VICINITY, THE ATLANTA CITY HALL
AND COURT HOUSE, THE CHURCH
OF THE IMMACULATE CONCEPTION,
ST. PHILIP'S EPISCOPAL CHURCH,
TRINITY METHODIST CHURCH, THE
SECOND BAPTIST CHURCH AND THE
CENTRAL PRESBYTERIAN CHURCH.

ERECTED BY
THE ATLANTA HISTORICAL SOCIETY,
THE FIVE CHURCHES NAMED
AND THE CITY OF ATLANTA
1945

Fulton County, Atlanta

LOCATION: City Hall, Mitchell Street	DATE: 1945	STYLE: Memorial wall
BUILDERS: The Atlanta Historical Society, the city of Atlanta, and the five churches saved by Father O'Reilly		

IN MEMORY
OF
FATHER THOMAS O'REILLY
WHO IN NOVEMBER 1864 BY HIS
COURAGEOUS PROTEST TO THE FEDERAL
FORCES PREPARING TO BURN AND
EVACUATE THE CITY SAVED FROM THE
CONFLAGRATION THE FOLLOWING
BUILDINGS THEN LOCATED IN THIS
VICINITY: THE ATLANTA CITY HALL
AND COURT HOUSE, THE CHURCH
OF THE IMMACULATE CONCEPTION,
ST. PHILIP'S EPISCOPAL CHURCH,
TRINITY METHODIST CHURCH, THE
SECOND BAPTIST CHURCH AND THE
CENTRAL PRESBYTERIAN CHURCH.

ERECTED BY
THE ATLANTA HISTORICAL SOCIETY,
THE FIVE CHURCHES NAMED
AND THE CITY OF ATLANTA
1945

Above the inscription is the Seal of the City of Atlanta, which contains: a Phoenix rising from the flames; the word "RESURGENS"; the date 1847, the year the city was founded; and the date 1865, the year of its rebirth.

Fulton County, Atlanta

LOCATION: Glenwood Avenue at I-20	DATE: 1902 (Trimpi, p. 53)
STYLE: Upright cannon barrel on a stone block	

IN MEMORY OF

MAJ. GEN'L WM. H. T. WALKER

C. S. A.

BORN NOV. 26, 1816.

KILLED ON THIS SPOT,

JULY 22, 1864.

The inscription states that Gen. Walker was "killed on this spot." The monument was originally on a nearby hill, and was moved to the present location in the 1930s (The Civil War Picket, June 19, 2011, which attributes the information to Henry Bryant, chairman of the Battle of Atlanta Commemorative Organization).

Fulton County, Atlanta

LOCATION: Rhodes Hall, Peachtree Street	DATE: 1905	STYLE: Stained-glass windows
BUILDER: Amos Rhodes	FABRICATOR: Von Gerichten Art Glass Company, Columbus, Ohio	

DUM SPIRO SPERO

SIC SEMPER TYRANNIS

The nine stained-glass windows in three panels in Rhodes Hall depict four significant scenes from the history of the Confederacy. On the left are the inauguration of President Davis and the bombardment of Fort Sumter. In the center is the Battle of Manassas. On the right, we see Lee and his men at Appomattox.

Stained-glass portraits of prominent Confederate military and civilian leaders accompany the scenes. The windows are topped with seals of the thirteen Confederate states (including Kentucky and Missouri).

Amos Rhodes was the founder of Rhodes Furniture Company. The house was built in 1904. It is now the headquarters of the Georgia Trust for Historic Preservation.

A small window, hidden in a closet beneath the stairs, shows the Confederate Battle Flag, a regimental flag of blue with a circle of stars, a shield with the St. Andrew's cross, a bugle, and a canteen inscribed with "C.S.A."

The cryptic location of this window represents the sentiment expressed in the new century that the Cause should be remembered but the time had come to move on. "It is time to put the flags away," as the expression went.

This information was provided by the Georgia Trust.

Fulton County, Atlanta

LOCATION: Piedmont Hospital, Peachtree Road	**DATE:** 1944
STYLE: Memorial stone	**BUILDER:** The Atlanta Historical Society

THIS MEMORIAL
TO
AMERICAN VALOR
IS DEDICATED TO THE PARTICIPANTS
IN THE
BATTLE OF PEACHTREE CREEK
JULY 20, 1864
ON THIS THE 80TH ANNIVERSARY OF
THE FIRST
OF THE FOUR CONFLICTS FOR THE
POSSESSION
OF ATLANTA

ERECTED BY
THE ATLANTA HISTORICAL SOCIETY
1944

On the rear of the memorial an inscription presents a summary of the Confederate attack.

AT THIS POINT ABOUT 4:30 P.M.
THE BATTLE OF PEACHTREE CREEK
BEGAN WHEN CONFEDERATE
TROOPS
OF BATE'S, WALKER'S AND MANEY'S
DIVISIONS OF LT. GEN. W. J.
HARDEE'S
CORPS ATTACKED NEWTON'S
DIVISION
OF THE FEDERAL FOURTH CORPS,
MAJ.
GEN. O. O. HOWARD, COMMANDING.
THE CONFLICT RANGED WESTWARD
TO HOWELL MILL ROAD WITH SUC-
CESSIVE ASSAULTS BY THE
CONFED-
ERATE FORCES OF LORING'S AND OF
WALTHALL'S DIVISIONS OF LT. GEN.
A. P. STEWART'S CORPS, UPON THE
DIVISIONS OF WARD, GEARY AND
WILLIAMS OF THE FEDERAL
TWENTIETH
CORPS, MAJ. GEN. JOSEPH HOOKER
COMMANDING.

Similar in spirit to the Peachtree Battle Avenue marker of 1935, this stone monument honors the men who fought on both sides of the Battle of Peachtree Creek.

ON THIS HISTORIC GROUND WHERE
CONFEDERATE SOLDIERY, DEFENDING
ATLANTA, MET AND DISPUTED THE
SOUTHWARD ADVANCE OF FEDERAL
TROOPS ALONG PEACHTREE ROAD.
JULY 19TH 1864.
THIS MEMORIAL IS A TRIBUTE TO
AMERICAN VALOR,
WHICH THEY OF THE BLUE AND
THEY OF THE GRAY HAD AS A
COMMON HERITAGE
FROM THEIR FOREFATHERS OF
1776,
AND TO THE PERVADING SPIRIT
THEREOF WHICH, IN THE DAYS OF
1898 AND
THE GREAT WORLD CONFLICT OF
1917 — 1918,
PERFECTED THE REUNION OF THE
NORTH AND THE SOUTH.
ERECTED BY THE OLD GUARD OF ATLANTA
DEDICATED BY ATLANTA POST NO
AMERICAN LEGION

Fulton County, Atlanta

LOCATION: Peachtree Battle Avenue, near the intersection with Peachtree Road		
DATE: 1935	STYLE: Memorial stone	BUILDER: Old Guard of Atlanta

ON THIS HISTORIC GROUND WHERE
CONFEDERATE SOLDIERY, DEFENDING
ATLANTA, MET AND DISPUTED THE
SOUTHWARD ADVANCE OF FEDERAL
TROOPS ALONG PEACHTREE ROAD,
JULY 19TH 1864.
THIS MEMORIAL IS A TRIBUTE TO
AMERICAN VALOR,
WHICH THEY OF THE BLUE AND
THEY OF THE GRAY HAD AS A
COMMON HERITAGE
FROM THEIR FOREFATHERS OF
1776,
AND TO THE PERVADING SPIRIT
THEREOF WHICH, IN THE DAYS OF
1898 AND
THE GREAT WORLD CONFLICT OF
1917-1918,
PERFECTED THE REUNION OF THE
NORTH AND THE SOUTH.
ERECTED BY THE OLD GUARD OF ATLANTA.
DEDICATED BY ATLANTA POST NO. 1,
AMERICAN LEGION.
1935.

At the top of the stone are carvings of a kepi and a steel helmet, along with a Civil War-era rifle musket crossed with a more modern rifle.

This monument is unique in Georgia in that it honors American soldiers on both sides of the Civil War, the veterans of the Spanish-American War and those of World War I.

Fulton County, Campbellton

LOCATION: Church Street and Cochran Road	DATE: 1936
STYLE: Stone structure with a bronze plaque	BUILDERS: UDC and WPA

SITE OF

THE

CAMPBELL COUNTY COURT HOUSE

WHERE, IN JUNE 1867, THE WIDOW

OF CAPTAIN T.C. GLOVER CALLED

A REUNION OF THE SURVIVORS

OF COMPANY A, 21ST GEORGIA, C.S.A.

WHO AGREED TO HOLD ANNUAL

MEETINGS.

W.P.A.   1936   U.D.C.

This monument is one of three in an area that was in Campbell County prior to the merger of Campbell into Fulton, the others being in Fairburn and Palmetto.

GEORGIA'S CONFEDERATE MONUMENTS

Fulton County, Fairburn

LOCATION: City Cemetery, West Broad Street	**DATE**: 1930	
STYLE: Column with a Corinthian capital	**BUILDER**: UDC	

IN MEMORY

OF OUR

CONFEDERATE SOLDIERS

1861–1865

ERECTED BY

CAMPBELL COUNTY

U.D.C. CHAPTER

JAN. 1, 1930

At the time of the monument's dedication, Fairburn was the seat of Campbell County. Two years later Campbell County was abolished and the territory was absorbed into Fulton County. This monument is one of three in an area that was in Campbell County prior to the merger of Campbell into Fulton, the others being in Palmetto and Campbellton. The actual dedication was June 3, 1930 (McKenney).

This monument was originally located on a railroad right-of-way near its current home. It was moved to the cemetery in the late 1940s (UDC 2002).

The dates of the war are repeated opposite the main inscription. A marble ball rests atop the capital.

The column is made of marble.

Fulton County, Palmetto

LOCATION: Main Street and Toombs Street	**DATE**: 1906	**STYLE**: Marble column
BUILDER: UDC	**FABRICATOR**: Fairburn Marble Co.	

ERECTED BY THE
DAUGHTERS
OF THE
CONFEDERACY
A. D. 1906.

C. S. A

The inscriptions on the sides honor two companies.

COMPANY I,
2ND REGIMENT
GEORGIA
VOLUNTEERS,
WHEELER'S CAVALRY.

COMPANY C,
19TH INFANTRY,
GEORGIA
VOLUNTEERS.
COMMANDED BY
COL. TOM JOHNSON.
COL. R. B. HOGAN.

On the front face is a carving of a rifle crossed with a flagpole, around which is draped a flag of uncertain design. Beneath this carving is a wreath encircling the letters "U.D.C." At the base of the column is another wreath with "61" to the left and "65" to the right.

A Georgia Historical Commission tablet at the site tells of events that took place in wartime Palmetto. Hood's Army of Tennessee was headquartered there in September 1864. President Jefferson Davis visited the army that month. It was there that Hardee was relieved of his command. Finally, it was from Palmetto that Hood embarked on his disastrous Tennessee Campaign.

This monument is one of three in an area that was in Campbell County prior to the merger of Campbell into Fulton, the others being in Fairburn and Campbellton.

The monument's cost was $1,500 (McKenney).

GEORGIA'S CONFEDERATE MONUMENTS

Fulton County, Roswell

LOCATION: Park at Sloan Street and Vickery Street	**DATE**: 2000
STYLE: Fluted column, broken at the top	**BUILDER**: SCV

THE ROSWELL MILLS WORKERS
MONUMENT

GIFT TO THE CITY OF ROSWELL
BY THE ROSWELL MILLS CAMP
No. 1547
SONS OF CONFEDERATE VETERANS
JULY 8, 2000

ROSWELL MANUFACTURING
COMPANY
INCORPORATED DECEMBER 1839
BY ROSWELL KING
COTTON MILLS EXPANDED BY
BARRINGTON KING

IVY WOOLEN MILL
ESTABLISHED 1857 BY JAMES
AND THOMAS KING

SUPPLIERS OF CLOTH AND YARN
TO THE CONFEDERATE
GOVERNMENT 1861–1864

SEIZED BY FEDERAL CAVALRY
JULY 5, 1864
WHILE IVY MILL UNDER THE FLAG
OF FRANCE

MILLS BURNED JULY 6, 1864

COTTON MILL REBUILT AND
OPERATED UNDER
VARIOUS OWNERS UNTIL
DESTROYED BY FIRE 1926

TO THE MEN OF ROSWELL
AND COBB COUNTY WHO SERVED
THE CONFEDERATE STATES
OF AMERICA

THE ROSWELL BATTALION
LOCAL DEFENSE TROOPS

CO. E. COBB'S LEGION CAVALRY
BATTALION
"ROSWELL TROOPERS"

CO. H. 7TH GEORGIA
VOLUNTEER INFANTRY
"ROSWELL GUARDS"

HONORING THE MEMORY OF
THE FOUR HUNDRED WOMEN,
CHILDREN, AND MEN
MILLWORKERS OF ROSWELL
WHO WERE CHARGED WITH TREASON
AND DEPORTED BY TRAIN
TO THE NORTH
BY INVADING FEDERAL FORCES
JULY 10, 1864

The base contains the SCV logo, the Southern Cross of Honor, cotton bolls, and a garland of leaves and flowers.

Gilmer County, Ellijay

LOCATION: Veterans Memorial Park, Georgia Highway 5, south of downtown		
DATE: 2003	STYLE: Memorial stone	BUILDER: SCV

DEDICATED TO THE MEMORY
OF THE
CONFEDERATE SOLDIERS
OF GILMER COUNTY
1861–1865
DEO VINDICE

ERECTED BY: GILMER LIGHT GUARDS CAMP # 89
SONS OF CONFEDERATE VETERANS   2003

A very similar monument, just steps away from the Confederate monument, honors the men of Gilmer County who served in the Union Army in the Civil War. There are several monuments honoring men who served in the Confederate Army and in the United States Army in World War I, but only two which recognize Georgia men serving in the Union Army: here and in nearby Union County.

A battle flag and a Maltese cross are pictured above the inscription.

GEORGIA'S CONFEDERATE MONUMENTS

Glynn County, Brunswick

LOCATION: Hanover Park, Newcastle Street	DATE: 1903 (CMSA, p. 115)
STYLE: Statue of a soldier on a column	BUILDER: LMA

CONFEDERATE STATES
OF
AMERICA
1861 TO 1865.

LORD GOD OF HOSTS BE WITH US
YET,
LEST WE FORGET, LEST WE FORGET.

(From "Recessional" by Rudyard Kipling)

ERECTED
APRIL 26TH, 1902.
A TRIBUTE OF LOVE
FROM THE LADIES
MEMORIAL ASSOCIATION OF
BRUNSWICK, GEORGIA, TO THE
HEROES OF THE CONFEDERACY.
1861 TO 1865.

IN HONOR OF THE
CONFEDERATE SOLDIERS,
WHO DIED TO REPEL
UNCONSTITUTIONAL
INVASION, TO PROTECT THE
RIGHTS RESERVED TO THE
PEOPLE, TO PERPETUATE
FOR EVER THE SOVEREIGNTY
OF THE STATES.

GATHER THE SACRED
DUST OF WARRIORS
TRIED AND TRUE, WHO
BORE THE FLAG OF OUR
NATION'S TRUST; AND FELL
IN THE CAUSE, THOUGH
LOST, STILL JUST; AND
DIED FOR YOU AND ME.

(From "The March of the Deathless Dead"
by Abram J. Ryan)

The front face of the column contains a Confederate Battle Flag on an unbroken staff. "CSA" is carved beneath the flag. The soldier is standing at rest. The column and base appear to be marble, as well as the statue.

Gordon County, Calhoun

LOCATION: Park north of downtown on US Highway 41 at Georgia Highway 225

DATE: 1927 | STYLE: Two bronze statues on a stone archway

BUILDER: A committee of Calhoun citizens

FABRICATORS: W. L. Hillhouse and the J. L. Mott Iron Works

CONFEDERATE
MEMORIAL
BATTLE OF RESACA FOUGHT
NEAR HERE MAY 14 AND 15 1864

(Below the Confederate)

CALHOUN HONORS HER
WORLD WAR
HEROES
1917–1918

(Beneath the World War soldier)

Credit is given to the foundryman on small plate tacked to the stone underneath the Confederate:

THE J. L. MOTT
IRON WKS. N.Y.

COMMITTEE
MRS. ERNEST NEAL, CHAIR.
MRS. C. C. HARLAN, TREAS.
MRS. J. B. ERWIN
J. C. CARLINGTON, MAYOR
W. L. HILLHOUSE, BLDR.
1927

This monument is one of the few in Georgia made of bronze and one of the few that combine memorials to Confederate soldiers and Georgians serving in the United States army in World War I. It is also unusual for the names of the committee members to be shown on the monument itself; most often only an organization is named, not individuals. The World War soldier does not look like a doughboy, but more like a soldier in the Spanish-American War. The tablet is clear even if the soldier looks out of place. Hillhouse, the fabricator of the arch, was also responsible for the arch in the Resaca Confederate Cemetery.

The Confederate is standing in the charge bayonet position.

The inscriptions below the soldiers are carved on marble stones placed in the columns on each side of the arch.

Gordon County, Resaca

LOCATION: Confederate Cemetery, Confederate Cemetery Road	**DATE**: Arch was built in 1911.

STYLE: Stone arch at cemetary entrance, a stone cross in the center, and a memorial stone

BUILDER: Gordon County was responsible for the memorial stone.

FABRICATOR: W. L. Hillhouse was the designer and fabricator of the arch.

Above the arch:

RESACA CONFEDERATE CEMETERY

On a bronze tablet at the entrance:

THIS TABLET IS DEDICATED BY THE
ATLANTA CHAPTER OF THE UNITED
DAUGHTERS OF THE CONFEDERACY TO
THE MEMORY OF MISS MARY GREEN, WHO
ESTABLISHED THIS RESACA CEMETERY —
THE FIRST OF THIS STATE — FOR OUR
CONFEDERATE SOLDIERS.
MADE BY THE GEORGIA SCHOOL OF
TECHNOLOGY — W. P. A.

On the memorial stone:

GEORGIA
CONFEDERATE SOLDIERS
WE SLEEP HERE IN OBEDIENCE
TO LAW:
WHEN DUTY CALLED WE CAME:
WHEN COUNTRY CALLED WE
DIED.

ERECTED BY GORDON COUNTY

Inscribed on each side of cross:
TO THE UNKNOWN DEAD

The Georgia School of Technology was the official name for Georgia Tech from its founding in 1885 until 1948, when the name was changed to the Georgia Institute of Technology.

There is no information on the cross to indicate when and by whom it was made. A Georgia Historical Commission marker states that the cemetery itself was established "shortly after the war." A signboard outside the cemetery gives the date as 1866.

A marble block placed in the wall, at the arch, states that W. L. Hillhouse was the designer and builder and gives the date. Hillhouse was also the fabricator of the arch in nearby Calhoun.

Grady County, Cairo

LOCATION: Courthouse grounds, North Broad Street	DATE: 2001 (Wiggins)
STYLE: Obelisk	BUILDER: SCV (Wiggins)

IN MEMORY
OF THE
CONFEDERATE
SOLDIER
WHO SERVED
IN THE WAR
BETWEEN THE STATES
1861–1865

"THEY DIED
IN THE
CONSCIOUSNESS
OF DUTY
FAITHFULLY
PERFORMED"

ROBERT E. LEE

Seventy-two bricks containing the names of Confederate soldiers and their units are set around the base.

The SCV logo is engraved on one side. On the other are the letters "CSA" underneath crossed rifles.

The Ochlocknee Rifles Camp 1807 of the SCV is responsible for the construction of this monument (Wiggins).

IN HONOR
OF THE BRAVE
WHO FELL DEFENDING
THE RIGHT OF LOCAL
SELF-GOVERNMENT.

OUR CONFEDERATE DEAD

Greene County, Greensboro

LOCATION: Courthouse grounds, facing North Main Street	DATE: 1898
STYLE: Statue of a soldier on a round column	BUILDERS: UDC and LMA (McKenney)

OUR CONFEDERATE DEAD

IN HONOR
OF THE BRAVE
WHO FELL DEFENDING
THE RIGHT OF LOCAL
SELF-GOVERNMENT.

ERECTED
A.D. 1898,
BY THE WOMEN
OF GREENE COUNTY.

"FAITHFUL
UNTO DEATH."

1861–1865

The monument is 30 feet high and cost $2,000. The "Women of Greene County" referred to on the monument were members of the UDC and LMA working together (McKenney).

The quote is taken from Revelation 2:10: "Be thou faithful unto death, and I will give thee the Crown of Life" (King James Version).

Upright cannon barrels, breach down, form pilasters at the corners of the plinth. Crossed sabers decorate all four sides at the top of the plinth. Four stone cannon balls are placed around the column. The round column is unusual for a Georgia monument.

The soldier is standing at rest.

Greene County, Union Point

LOCATION: Lamb Avenue (US Highway 278)	DATE: 1874	STYLE: Obelisk

COMMEMORATING
THE SITE OF THE
FIRST REGIMENTAL
REUNION OF
CONFEDERATE VETERANS.

SURVIVORS OF THE
3RD. GEORGIA REGIMENT
MET AT THE
UNION POINT FAIR GROUNDS
JULY 30–31, 1874.

Crossed battle flags are engraved on the front face, above the inscriptions.

COMMEMORATING
THE SITE OF THE
FIRST REGIMENTAL
REUNION OF
CONFEDERATE VETERANS

SURVIVORS OF THE
3RD. GEORGIA REGIMENT
MET AT THE
UNION POINT FAIR GROUNDS
JULY 30 – 31, 1874.

COMMEMORATING
THE
CONFEDERATE WAYSIDE
HOME 1862-1864 WHOSE
ACTIVITIES WERE CARRIED
ON BY FOURTEEN WOMEN
OF UNION POINT.
W.P.A.   1936

Greene County, Union Point

LOCATION: Carlton Avenue and Thornton Street | **STYLE**: Boulder with a bronze tablet

(First marker)

THE TWO COMMITTEES
WHO ALTERNATED WEEKLY
IN CARRYING ON THE WAYSIDE HOME
(A list of sixteen names follows.)

(Second marker)

COMMEMORATING
THE
CONFEDERATE WAYSIDE
HOME 1862–1864. WHOSE
ACTIVITIES WERE CARRIED
ON BY FOURTEEN WOMEN
OF UNION POINT.

W.P.A.   1936

The wayside home was established by the women of the town to offer food and a resting place for Confederate soldiers in transit. Union Point is on the railroad between Atlanta and Augusta. There is a collection of documents on the Union Point Wayside Home at the University of North Carolina (Wayside Home Register, collection no. 3588-z, Southern Historical Collection, Wilson Library, University of North Carolina at Chapel Hill. Information obtained from the University's website (www.lib.unc.edu/mss/inv/u/Wayside_Home.html, accessed November 2011.) A similar monument is located in Millen (Jenkins County) as a memorial to the wayside home there. Two monuments in Kingston (Bartow County) commemorate the wayside home in that community.

The second marker honoring the women of the Union Point Wayside Home is located at Sibley Avenue and Fluker Street. This marker also consists of a bronze tablet on a stone set on the ground.

There was also a wayside home in Albany, but there is no memorial (CSMA, p. 84).

Gwinnett County, Lawrenceville

LOCATION: Old courthouse grounds, on the Pike Street side of the courthouse	
DATE: 1993	STYLE: Tall stone slab flanked by two shorter slabs
	BUILDERS: SCV and UDC

1861–1865
LEST WE FORGET

IN REMEMBRANCE
OF THE CITIZENS
OF GWINNETT
COUNTY WHO
HONORABLY SERVED
THE CONFEDERATE
STATES OF AMERICA

"ANY PEOPLE WITH
CONTEMPT FOR THEIR
HERITAGE HAVE LOST
FAITH IN THEMSELVES
AND NO NATION CAN LONG
SURVIVE WITHOUT PRIDE
IN ITS TRADITIONS."
SIR WINSTON CHURCHILL

PRESENTED BY
SONS OF CONFEDERATE VETERANS CAMP 96
AND
UNITED DAUGHTERS OF THE CONFEDERACY
CHAPTER 2365
1993

This was the first polychromatic monument built in Georgia. It contains a First National Flag in full color, with eleven stars, behind a mustached soldier in gray, standing at rest. Above the flag is the Great Seal of the Confederacy.

IN REMEMBRANCE
OF THE CITIZENS
OF GWINNETT
COUNTY WHO
HONORABLY SERVED
THE CONFEDERATE
STATES OF AMERICA

1861 — 1865
LEST WE FORGET

"ANY PEOPLE WITH
CONTEMPT FOR THEIR
HERITAGE HAVE LOST
FAITH IN THEMSELVES
AND NO NATION CAN LONG
SURVIVE WITHOUT PRIDE
IN IT'S TRADITIONS."
SIR WINSTON CHURCHILL

Gwinnett County, Lawrenceville

LOCATION: Fallen Heroes Memorial, at the Justice and Administration Center, Langley Drive

| **DATE:** 2003 | **STYLE:** Memorial stones arranged in an arc | **BUILDER:** Gwinnett County |

FABRICATORS: Breedlove Land Planning, Inc. (landscape architect), Ponder & Ponder (architect), Vic McCallum (eagle sculptor), Project Earth Landscape Management Services, Inc. (general contractor), and Keystone Memorials, Inc. (granite installation)

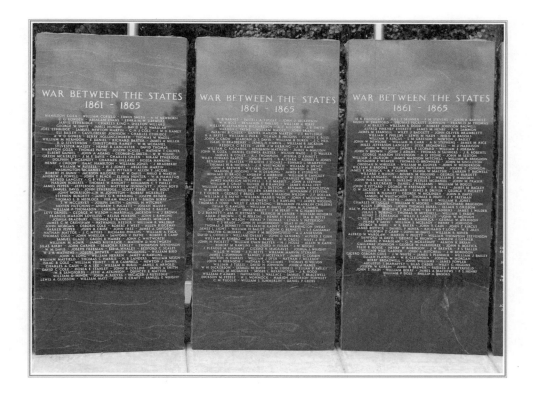

Three of the thirteen markers are devoted to the War Between the States. The author's rough count indicates some 500 names, about three times as many as all the others combined.

The different slabs are dedicated to the people of the county who lost their lives in war and in other circumstances.

One slab honors the "NATIVE PEOPLE WHO WERE THE FIRST TO LOVE THIS GREAT LAND." After that the markers take us from the American Revolution through all the nation's wars, including the global war on terrorism, then finally to policemen, firemen, and other county employees killed in the line of duty.

Each of these slabs lists the names of the "Fallen Heroes."

Hall County, Gainesville

LOCATION: Town square in downtown Gainesville, facing Washington Street

DATE: 1909	STYLE: Bronze statue of a soldier on a stone pedestal	BUILDER: UDC

FABRICATOR: McNeel Marble Co. (McNeel Memorials)

TO THE DEFENDERS OF
THE CONFEDERACY,
PATRIOTS
THE RECORD OF WHOSE FORTITUDE AND
HEROISM IN THE SERVICE OF THEIR
COUNTY IS THE PROUD HERITAGE OF
A LOYAL POSTERITY.
"TELL YE YOUR CHILDREN OF IT, AND
LET YOUR CHILDREN TELL THEIR CHILDREN
AND THEIR CHILDREN ANOTHER GENERATION."

(Joel 1:3, King James Version)

OUR CONFEDERATE SOLDIERS

ERECTED BY THE
LONGSTREET CHAPTER
DAUGHTERS OF THE CONFEDERACY

DEDICATED TO SOUTHERN CONVICTIONS
CONSECRATED TO SOUTHERN VALOR

UNVEILED JUNE 7, 1909.

1861 C.S.A. 1865

According to McKenney, a Chicago firm (unnamed) made the statue for $2,500. The speaker at the dedication was Hooper Alexander. Alexander also spoke at the DeKalb ceremony and wrote the inscription for that county's monument.

On the front, beneath the soldier, is a Confederate Battle Flag. On the rear is the First National, with a circle of thirteen stars.

The soldier is standing in the charge bayonet position.

McNeel Memorials includes this monument in its list, but only the base is the work of McNeel.

GENERAL
JAMES LONGSTREET, C.S.A.
1 – 1904

Hall County, Gainesville

LOCATION: Park at Park Hill Drive and Longstreet Place	DATE: 2001
STYLE: Bronze statue of General Longstreet on a low pedestal	BUILDER: UDC
SCULPTOR: Gregory Johnson	

GENERAL
JAMES LONGSTREET, C. S. A.
1821–1904

THIS MONUMENT
ENDOWED BY THE L. DENTON HADAWAY ESTATE
DESIGNED AND SCULPTED BY GREGORY JOHNSON
ERECTED IN 2001 BY THE
GENERAL JAMES LONGSTREET CHAPTER #46
UNITED DAUGHTERS OF THE CONFEDERACY ®

Near the statue is a bronze tablet, erected by the WPA and the UDC in 1936, to mark the site of General Longstreet's home.

Hall County, Oakwood

LOCATION: Redwine Cemetery, Poplar Springs Road and Robert Wood Johnson Drive

DATE: 1935 (Wiggins) | STYLE: Stone monument

HONOR THE BRAVE

CO. D. 27TH. GA. REG.

C.S.A

1861–1865

THEY WERE MEN
WHOM POWER COULD NOT CORRUPT
WHOM DEATH COULD NOT TERRIFY
WHOM DEFEAT COULD NOT DISHONOR,
THEY WERE FAITHFUL TO THE TEACH-
INGS OF THEIR FATHERS,
DIED IN THE PERFORMANCE OF DUTY
AND HAVE GLORIFIED A FALLEN CAUSE.

*(This is a variation of a passage from a speech by William Henry Trescot.
See the entry for the Cartersville monument in Bartow County.)*

TO THE WOMEN
OF THE CONFEDER-
ACY WHOSE TRUTH,
CONSTANCY AND
LOYALTY SHALL
REMAIN UNTO THEM
AND THEIR CHIL-
DREN AS A CROWN
OF GLORY AND A
DIADEM OF BEAUTY.

The monument is decorated with images of the Southern Cross of Honor, a flag, crossed rifles, a canteen, two fleurs-de-lis, and a laurel branch and wreath. (The flag is an odd combination of the First National and Second National. There is a St. Andrew's cross in the canton, but the rest of the hoist and the fly have horizontal stripes.)

The monument is made of marble.

Hancock County, Sparta

LOCATION: Park in front of the courthouse, Court Street and Broad Street		
DATE: 1881	**STYLE:** Obelisk	**BUILDER:** LMA
FABRICATOR: Muldoon Monument Co. (McKenney)		

"GEORGIA'S
WAS THE WORD."

"AND THEIRS
THE WILL TO DIE."

"IN MEMORIAM."

OUR
CONFEDERATE
DEAD

ERECTED BY THE
LADIES
MEMORIAL ASSOCIATION
OF HANCOCK COUNTY
1881.

The marble obelisk was originally erected without a base. It was placed on a granite base and rededicated on Confederate Memorial Day, 1884. The cost was just under $1,000 (McKenney).

On the north side the Great Seal of the Confederacy is carved in the plinth. The south side contains a carving of crossed sabers in a festoon of foliage. Beneath this is a carving in high relief of a Confederate soldier. This is a unique feature among Georgia monuments.

The soldier is standing at rest.

Harris County, Hamilton

LOCATION: Park in the center of town, facing Barnes Mill Road	DATE: 1910 (McKenney)
STYLE: Statue of a soldier on a column	BUILDER: LMA (McKenney)
FABRICATOR: McNeel Marble Co. (McNeel Memorials)	

OUR CONFEDERATE
SOLDIERS
1861–1865

"FATE DENIED THEM
VICTORY, BUT CROWNED
THEM WITH GLORIOUS
IMMORTALITY."

The monument is the last one in Georgia built solely by a ladies' memorial association (McKenney).

On the front of the column, immediately below the statue, are the letters "CSA." At the base of the column are two carvings. One displays crossed flags, the Confederate Battle Flag and the Second National. The other carving, in mid relief, depicts a camp scene: three stacked rifles from which hangs a canteen, with trees in the background. There are stone cannonballs on the corners of the plinth.

The soldier is standing at rest.

Hart County, Hartwell

LOCATION: Courthouse grounds, facing East Howell Street	**DATE**: 1908 (McKenney)
STYLE: Statue of a soldier on a column	**BUILDER**: UDC (McKenney)
FABRICATOR: McNeel Marble Co. (McNeel Memorials)	

IN LOVING MEMORY
OF OUR HART COUNTY
SOLDIERS

The statue was unveiled on July 28, 1908, by the Hartwell Chapter of the United Daughters of the Confederacy (McKenney).

On the front of the shaft is a torn battle flag on a broken staff. The letters "CSA" are carved in pediments in the front and rear just below the statue. The dates of the war are inscribed, also on the front and rear, on pediments above the plinth.

The soldier is standing at rest.

Heard County, Franklin

LOCATION: Town square, facing Davis Street	**DATE**: 1999
STYLE: Memorial stone	**BUILDER**: UDC

1861   1865

WAR BETWEEN THE STATES
HEARD COUNTY SOLDIERS

INFANTRY	CO.	REG.
	G	7TH
	E	19TH
	K	34TH
	D	35TH
	I	41ST
	D	53RD
	K	56TH
CAVALRY	E	10TH

TO THE HONOR AND GLORY

DEDICATED BY THE
UNITED DAUGHTERS
OF THE CONFEDERACY
HEARD COUNTY
CHAPTER # 2587
APRIL 26, 1999

A Maltese cross is carved on the slanted top of the monument, between "1861" and "1865."

GEORGIA'S CONFEDERATE MONUMENTS

Henry County, McDonough

LOCATION: Courthouse grounds, facing Keys Ferry Street	**DATE:** 1911 (Widener)
STYLE: Statue of a soldier on a column	**BUILDER:** UDC
FABRICATOR: McNeel Marble Co. (McNeel Memorials)	

TO OUR CONFEDERATE SOLDIERS,
THOSE WHO FELL IN FIERCEST
FIGHTING AND SLEEP BENEATH
THE SOD OF EVERY SOUTHERN STATE.
THOSE WHO HAVE PASSED AWAY
IN THE AFTER YEARS OF PEACE,
AND WHOSE ASHES NOW HALLOW
OLD HENRY'S HILL SIDES,
THOSE WHO LIKE A BENEDICTION,
STILL LIMP IN OUR MIDST.
MAY GOD PRESERVE FOREVER IN
OUR HEARTS, THEIR MEMORY AND
IN ALL MINDS, A KNOWLEDGE OF
THEIR MOTIVES AND THEIR CAUSE.

COMRADES

TO OUR
CONFEDERATE
DEAD

ERECTED BY THE
CHAS. T. ZACHRY CHAPTER
UNITED DAUGHTERS
OF THE CONFEDERACY.
1910.

"CSA" is inscribed on the pediments, front and rear, at the top of the plinth. Engraved on each of the side pediments is "1861–1865." Crossed rifles decorate one side of the plinth, crossed flags the other.

The soldier is standing at rest.

Houston County, Perry

LOCATION: Courthouse grounds, Carroll Street	DATE: 1908 (McKenney)
STYLE: Statue of a soldier on a column	BUILDER: UDC
FABRICATOR: McNeel Marble Co. (McNeel Memorials)	

IN HONOR OF
THE MEN OF HOUSTON COUNTY,
WHO SERVED IN THE ARMY
OF THE CONFEDERATE
STATES OF AMERICA.
"THOSE WHO FOUGHT AND
LIVED,
AND THOSE WHO FOUGHT AND
DIED."

ERECTED BY THE DAUGHTERS
OF THE CONFEDERACY.

COMRADES

TO OUR
CONFEDERATE
DEAD

MAY THIS SHAFT EVER
CALL TO MEMORY,
"THE STORY OF THE GLORY
OF THE MEN WHO WORE THE
GRAY."
*(From "The Men Who Wore the Gray"
by Abram J. Ryan)*

A. D. 1907

HOUSTON COUNTY
CHAPTER
U. D. C.

The monument was dedicated April 27, 1908; the cost was approximately $2,400. The original location was at an intersection in Perry (US 41 and 341 as the highways were later designated). The relocation to the courthouse grounds was in 1948 or thereabouts, when the current courthouse was built (McKenney).

It appears that the soldier is placed on the column facing in the wrong direction. The inscriptions below the soldier's right (the first four quoted above) seem designed for the front, not the side. The statue is similar to the one in LaFayette (Walker County), also by McNeel, and is not typical of the company's work.

The pediments at the top of the plinth are engraved with "1861–1865" on the front and rear and "CSA" on the sides. Crossed rifles decorate the front of the plinth; a Confederate Battle Flag with a broken staff is on the rear.

The soldier is standing at rest.

Irwin County, Irwinville

LOCATION: Jefferson Davis Historic Site, Jeff Davis Road	**DATE:** 1935
STYLE: Bust of Jefferson Davis on a pedestal	**BUILDERS:** State of Georgia and UDC
SCULPTOR: Laurence Tomkins	

JEFFERSON DAVIS

PRESIDENT
OF THE
CONFEDERATE STATES
OF AMERICA
1861–1865

ON THIS SPOT
MAY 10, 1865
PRESIDENT JEFFERSON DAVIS
WAS MADE A
PRISONER OF WAR
BY FEDERAL TROOPS

ERECTED BY THE
STATE OF GEORGIA
EUGENE TALMADGE,
GOVERNOR
IN THE YEAR 1935

SPONSORED BY MARY V.
HENDERSON
CHAPTER AND THE GEORGIA
DIVISION
OF THE UNITED DAUGHTERS OF
THE
CONFEDERACY

On the front of the pedestal is an interesting carving, showing Davis, erect and dignified, standing with two of his Union captors.

The Confederate Battle Flag is on one side of the pedestal, the First National on the other. The sculptor is credited below the First National.

The rear contains a carving of a battle scene and the names of persons responsible for the work.

Irwin County, Ocilla

LOCATION: Courthouse grounds, facing Second Street	**DATE:** 1911
STYLE: Statue of a soldier on a column	**BUILDER:** UDC
FABRICATOR: McNeel Marble Co. (McNeel Memorials)	

IN MEMORY OF
OUR
CONFEDERATE
SOLDIERS

ERECTED BY THE
MARY V. HENDERSON CHAPTER,
UNITED DAUGHTERS
OF THE CONFEDERACY,
TO THE
CONFEDERATE SOLDIERS
OF OUR BELOVED SOUTHLAND.
1911.

"TELL IT AS YOU MAY,
IT NEVER CAN BE TOLD!
SING IT AS YOU WILL
IT NEVER CAN BE SUNG
THE STORY OF THE GLORY
OF THE MEN WHO WORE THE
GRAY."

*(From "The Men Who Wore the Gray"
by Abram J. Ryan)*

"SILENTLY THIS STONE
PROCLAIMS THE DEATHLESS
FAME OF THOSE WHO FOUGHT
AND FELL.
HONOR TO HEROES IS GLORY
TO OUR GOD AND OUR
COUNTRY."

1861–1865

This monument has an unusual feature: cannon barrels protruding from the front and rear of the plinth. On the front face the barrel is set between crossed sabers. On the column, above the plinth, are crossed flags, the Confederate Battle Flag and the Third National, with "1861" above the flags and "1865" below.

The monument was moved to present location from a downtown intersection around 1940. The monument is 30 feet tall (McKenney). A bronze tablet states that the monument was restored in 1999 by the SCV Camp 682.

The soldier is standing at rest.

GEORGIA'S CONFEDERATE MONUMENTS

Jackson County, Commerce

LOCATION: Park on South Elm Street	**DATE**: 1941
STYLE: Stone pillar	**BUILDER**: UDC

DEVOTED IN
THEIR LABORS
FERVENT IN
THEIR HOPES
VALIANT IN
SACRIFICE

THE PRINCIPLES
FOR WHICH
THEY FOUGHT
LIVE
ETERNALLY

DEDICATED
TO THE
WOMEN
AND
VETERANS
OF THE
WAR
BETWEEN
THE STATES
1861–1865

J. E. B. STUART CHAPTER U. D. C.
A. D. 1941

The dedicatory inscription is repeated on the opposite side, above the names of the UDC members responsible for the monument.

The top of the pillar contains engravings on all four sides. One carving consists of a torch wrapped in a garland. A second carving shows a rifle crossed with a saber, also wrapped in a garland. There are two identical carvings of a Confederate Battle Flag, a Southern Cross of Honor, and a garland.

Near the monument is a black marble bench, commemorating the 100th anniversary of the UDC chapter.

Jackson County, Jefferson

LOCATION: Center of town, Sycamore Street	**DATE:** 1911
STYLE: Column topped with the Southern Cross of Honor	**BUILDER:** UDC
FABRICATOR: McNeel Marble Co. (McNeel Memorials)	

"LEST WE FORGET."

ERECTED BY
U. D. C. CHAPTER 1217,
JEFFERSON, GA., 1911.

COMRADES

"TO OUR
CONFEDERATE
SOLDIERS."

The dedication was held on Confederate Memorial Day, 1911. A statue of a soldier originally stood on the column. It was toppled in an accident in 1940 while preparations were being made for a speech by the postmaster general regarding the issuance of a stamp honoring Crawford W. Long. The statue was replaced by the cross (McKenney).

One face of the plinth displays the Confederate Battle Flag. On the opposite side are crossed rifles. There are four pediments above the plinth: two contain the dates of the war and two "CSA."

The monument was originally in the median of Sycamore Street but was later moved a short distance to its present location between the sidewalk and a parking lot. The author photographed the monument in its original location in 1991.

Wiggins contains a postcard photograph showing the monument as originally constructed, with the statue.

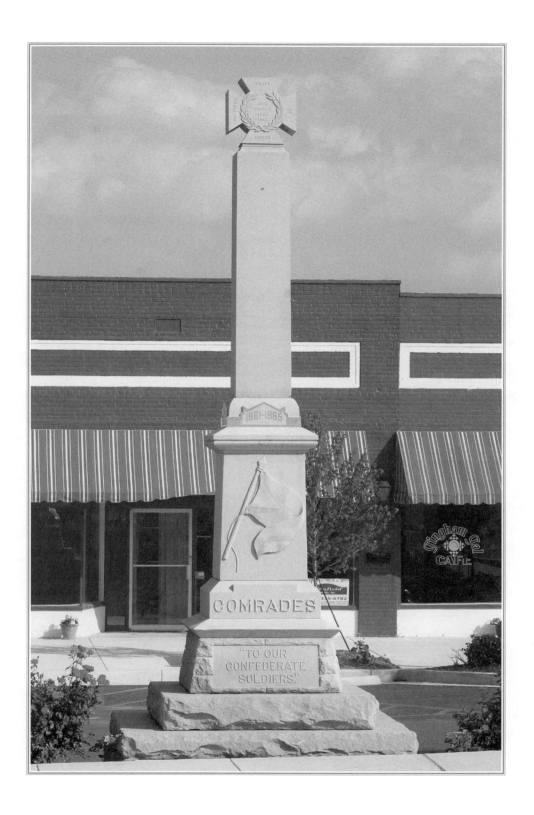

GEORGIA'S CONFEDERATE MONUMENTS

Jackson County, Jefferson

LOCATION: Center of town, Sycamore Street	STYLE: Bronze statue on a stone pedestal
DATE: 2011	BUILDERS: SCV and Friends of the Monument
SCULPTORS: Don Haugen and Teena Stearn (brochure printed for the unveiling ceremony)	

1861–1865

DEDICATED IN 2011 BY
SONS OF
CONFEDERATE
VETERANS
THE INTERNATIONAL SCV
THE GEORGIA DIVISION SCV
JACKSON COUNTY
VOLUNTEERS
SCV CAMP 94 JEFFERSON
FRIENDS OF THE MONUMENT

DEDICATED TO THE VALOR OF
JACKSON COUNTY
TROOPS
THAT SERVED THE
CONFEDERATE STATES
OF AMERICA

IN 2008
THE CITY OF JEFFERSON
AND
HISTORIC PRESERVATION COMMISSION
APPROVED THE REPLACEMENT OF THE
CSA STATUE BROKEN IN 1940

The statue was unveiled on October 1, 2011. Don Haugen also sculpted the statue in Paulding County, dedicated eight months after this one.

The granite base is the work of Baston Monuments of Elberton (brochure from the dedication ceremony).

Crossed cannon barrels and the SCV logo decorate the base.

The soldier is standing at rest.

Jasper County, Monticello

LOCATION: Town square, across West Green Street from the courthouse	**DATE**: 1910
STYLE: Statues of two soldiers, an infantryman and a cavalryman at the base of an obelisk	
BUILDER: UDC (McKenney)	**FABRICATOR**: McNeel Marble Co. (McNeel Memorials)

TO THE
CONFEDERATE SOLDIERS
OF JASPER COUNTY,
THE RECORD OF WHOSE
SUBLIME SELF-SACRIFICE
AND UNDYING DEVOTION
TO DUTY, IN THE SERVICE
OF THEIR COUNTRY,
IS THE PROUD HERITAGE
OF A LOYAL POSTERITY.

"IN LEGEND AND LAY,
OUR HEROES IN GRAY,
SHALL FOREVER LIVE
OVER AGAIN FOR US."
(From "C.S.A." by Abram J. Ryan)

COMRADES

"CROWNS OF ROSES FADE,
CROWNS OF THORNS ENDURE.
CALVARIES AND CRUCIFIXIONS
TAKE DEEPEST HOLD OF
HUMANITY,
THE TRIUMPHS OF MIGHT
ARE TRANSIENT,
THEY PASS AND ARE
FORGOTTEN,
THE SUFFERINGS OF RIGHT
ARE GRAVEN DEEPEST ON THE
CHRONICLE OF NATIONS."
*(From Abram J. Ryan's prose introduction
to his poem "A Land without Ruins")*

On the face of the plinth behind the infantryman are crossed rifles; behind the cavalryman are crossed sabers. "CSA" is engraved on two of the four pediments above the surfaces with the inscriptions.

A band around the column has the dates of the war on one side and "'Gloria Victis'" on the other. An anchor and a flag decorate opposite surfaces of the column. The infantryman is standing at rest; the cavalryman is drawing his sword.

The monument's cost was $2,400, paid in full before the unveiling (McKenney).

GEORGIA'S CONFEDERATE MONUMENTS

Jeff Davis County, Hazlehurst

LOCATION: Courthouse grounds, facing Jeff Davis Street and South Tallahassee Street		
DATE: 1999	**STYLE:** Bust of Jefferson Davis on a pedestal	**BUILDER:** SCV
	SCULPTOR: Thomas Bruno	

JEFFERSON DAVIS

PRESIDENT

CONFEDERATE STATES OF AMERICA

1861

PRESENTED TO PRESERVE THE
MEMORY OF THE SACRIFICES OF
THE PEOPLE OF THE SOUTH
AS EXEMPLIFIED BY OUR PRESIDENT

APPLING GRAYS
SONS OF CONFEDERATE VETERANS
CAMP #918

LOCAL CONFEDERATE UNITS

APPLING GRAYS, COMPANY I, 27TH
GEORGIA INFANTRY

APPLING RANGERS, COMPANY F,
17TH GEORGIA INFANTRY

APPLING VOLUNTEERS, COMPANY B,
54TH GEORGIA INFANTRY

SATILLA RIFLES, COMPANY K, 54TH
GEORGIA INFANTRY

CAPT. BEN MILIKIN'S MILITIA

COMPANY F, 1ST SYMON'S RESERVES

COMPANY K, CLINCH'S 4TH GEORGIA
CAVALRY

CAPT. SILAS CROSBY'S MILITIA

*Information about Davis's career in the service
of the United States is summarized:*

U. S. SECRETARY OF WAR

U. S. SENATOR

U. S. CONGRESSMAN

It is worth noting that the Georgia county named after the Confederate president had no Confederate memorial until this was built, 134 years after the war.

One side displays carvings of five Confederate flags, with their names: the Confederate Battle Flag, the Third National, the Bonnie Blue, the Stars and Bars, and the Stainless Banner.

The Great Seal of the Confederacy is on the front; the SCV logo is on the rear. The sculptor is credited on the rear of the bust.

Jenkins County, Millen

LOCATION: Courthouse grounds, East Winthrope Avenue		**DATE:** 1909
STYLE: Statue of a soldier on a column		**BUILDER:** UDC
FABRICATOR: McNeel Marble Co. (McNeel Memorials)		

ERECTED JUNE 3RD. 1909.

BY

THE WAYSIDE HOME

CHAPTER. U.D.C.

IN HONOR OF OUR

CONFEDERATE SOLDIERS,

WHOM POWER COULD

NOT CORRUPT,

WHOM DEATH COULD

NOT TERRIFY,

WHOM DEFEAT COULD

NOT DISHONOR.

(This is a variation of a passage from a speech by William Henry Trescot. See the entry for the Cartersville monument in Bartow County.)

THESE WERE MEN WHO

BY THE SIMPLE MANHOOD

OF THEIR LIVES,

BY THEIR STRICT ADHERENCE

TO THE PRINCIPLES OF RIGHT,

BY THEIR SUBLIME COURAGE

AND UNSPEAKABLE SACRIFICES,

EVEN TO THE HEROISM OF DEATH,

HAVE PRESERVED FOR US,

THROUGH THE GLOOM OF DEFEAT,

A PRICELESS HERITAGE OF HONOR.

"FOR EACH SINGLE WRECK

IN THE WAR PATH OF MIGHT,

SHALL YET BE A ROCK IN

THE TEMPLE OF RIGHT."

(From "A Land without Ruins" by Abram J. Ryan)

THOSE WHO SERVED.

THOSE WHO FOUGHT.

THOSE WHO FELL.

COMRADES

THE

CONFEDERACY.

A small stone marker states that the statue was rededicated on June 13, 2009, by the UDC. A larger stone placed by the SCV praises those who served the Confederacy, including "those men of color who joined ranks…to defend from the invader the only home they had ever known."

The dates of the war are engraved on opposite pediments above the plinth, front and rear; "CSA" is engraved on the side pediments. On the sides of the plinth adjacent to the inscriptions are crossed flags and crossed rifles.

The soldier is standing at rest.

Jenkins County, Millen

LOCATION: Courthouse grounds, East Winthrope Avenue	
STYLE: Boulder with a bronze tablet	**BUILDER:** UDC

THIS BOULDER IS PLACED BY
THE WAYSIDE HOME CHAPTER
UNITED DAUGHTERS OF THE CONFEDERACY
OF JENKINS COUNTY, GEORGIA AND
THE MARGARET JONES CHAPTER
UNITED DAUGHTERS OF THE CONFEDERACY
OF BURKE COUNTY, GEORGIA
TO PERPETUATE THE NAME OF
THE WAYSIDE HOME
AND AS A MEMORIAL TO THE NOBLE WOMEN
WHO SERVED THERE WITH VALOR AND PATRIOTISM

THE WAYSIDE HOME
WAS ESTABLISHED, MAINTAINED AND OPERATED BY
THE WOMEN OF BURKE COUNTY, GEORGIA
(NOW BURKE AND JENKINS COUNTIES)
FOR THE COMFORT AND RELIEF
OF OUR CONFEDERATE SOLDIERS

THOSE WHO SERVED AS PRESIDENTS OF THE HOME WERE
MRS. ANN MacKENZIE
MRS. ELIZABETH JONES
MRS. RANSOM LEWIS
MRS. AMOS WHITEHEAD

The wayside home in Millen operated until 1864 when it was destroyed by Sherman's forces. The home was established for the care of soldiers who were "sick or wounded and unable to continue their journey" (Underwood, p. 108).

A similar monument is in Union Point (Greene County) in memory of the wayside home located in that community. See that entry for a brief discussion of wayside homes.

There was also a wayside home in Albany, but there is no memorial (CSMA, p. 84).

At the bottom of the tablet are the UDC insignia and the dates 1861 and 1864.

Johnson County, Wrightsville

LOCATION: Courthouse grounds, West Elm Street		
DATE: 2002 (Donald Johnson)	**STYLE:** Marble cross	**BUILDER:** SCV

IN HONOR OF THE MORE THAN 600
GALLANT SOLDIERS FROM JOHNSON COUNTY
WHO NOT FOR FAME, REWARD OR AMBITION
BUT SIMPLE OBEDIENCE TO DUTY
AS THEY UNDERSTOOD IT
THESE MEN SUFFERED ALL, SACRIFICED ALL
DARED ALL, AND DIED.
THEIR CAUSE WAS NOBLE AND JUST,
AND ALMIGHTY GOD ALONE SHALL BE
THEIR VINDICATOR.

BRAVELY THEY SACRIFICED
GRATEFULLY WE REMEMBER
BATTLEGROUND GUARDS CAMP 1941

According to Donald Johnson, the cost of the monument was $3,200. The Battleground Guards Camp raised the funds through private donations. Johnson is a member of this camp.

The first inscription is based partly on the inscription on the Confederate memorial at Arlington National Cemetery, written by Randolph Harrison McKim. A similar inscription is found on the monument in Oglethorpe County. The Paulding County monument contains the entire McKim quote. See that entry for more information.

The SCV logo, in color, is on each side of monument.

GEORGIA'S CONFEDERATE MONUMENTS

Johnson County, Wrightsville

LOCATION: Macon Road (Georgia Highway 57) and Tucker Church Road	
DATE: 2003 (James M. Blizzard, commander of the Johnson Greys Camp 1688)	
STYLE: Memorial stone	**BUILDER:** SCV
FABRICATOR: Memorial stone was made by the McDaniel Monument Co., East Dublin, Georgia.	

IN MEMORY
OF THE MEN AND WOMEN
OF THE CONFEDERATE STATES OF AMERICA

THOUGH TIME HAS PASSED AND YOU ARE GONE
WE THAT ARE HERE REMEMBER YOUR SONG.
"DIXIE"

MANY A MAN LEFT HIS HOME
TO FIGHT FOR FREEDOM AND SAVE HIS OWN.
THOUGH WAR WAS TOUGH FOR YOU ALL
YOU NEVER GAVE UP YOUR FREEDOM CALL.
YOU FOUGHT EACH DAY AS THOUGH YOUR LAST
TO CARRY ON YOUR SOUTHERN PAST.
AS WE READ YOUR WORDS OF WAR,
LET US REMEMBER WHAT IT WAS FOR.

SOUTHERN INDEPENDENCE
A TIME OF TRUTH

BY: CMDR. LEO E. KIGHT, JR.

SONS OF CONFEDERATE VETERANS
JOHNSON GREYS
CAMP 1688

LAND DONATED BY MR. AND MRS. THURSTON PRICE

Above the inscription are five flags: the Confederate Battle Flag, the Bonnie Blue, and the First, Second, and Third National flags.

Two brick and concrete walls flank the memorial stone. The bricks list the men of two local companies, the Johnson Greys (Company F, 14th Georgia Infantry) and the Battleground Guards (Company F, 48th Georgia Infantry). On the ground in front of the monument is a pad of dyed concrete, approximately 18 feet square, forming a Confederate Battle Flag in full color. According to Blizzard, the monument was dedicated on Confederate Memorial Day and cost approximately $3500. The members of the camp did much of the work themselves, including the pouring of the concrete Confederate Battle Flag.

Jones County, Gray

LOCATION: Courthouse grounds, West Clinton Street and South Jefferson Street

STYLE: Memorial stone

TO THOSE MEN OF
JONES COUNTY,
WHO GAVE THEIR
SERVICE IN THE
WAR BETWEEN THE
STATES, 1861–1865
AND IN THE WORLD
WAR, 1917–1918

Lamar County, Barnesville

LOCATION: Greenwood Cemetery, Lamar Street		
DATE: 1889 (McKenney)	**STYLE:** Obelisk	**BUILDER:** LMA

OUR
CONFEDERATE
DEAD

Above the inscription is a furled flag crossed with a rifle.

Lamar County, Barnesville

LOCATION: In the median of Main Street, south of Forsyth Street		
DATE: 1927 (McKenney)	**STYLE:** Memorial stone with a bronze tablet	**BUILDER:** UDC

IN MEMORY OF
WOMEN OF THE CONFEDERACY
1861–1865
BY
WILLIE HUNT SMITH CHAPTER, U.D.C.
BARNESVILLE, GA.

GEORGIA'S CONFEDERATE MONUMENTS

Laurens County, Dublin

LOCATION: A triangle formed by Academy Avenue and Bellevue Avenue	
DATE: 1912 (McKenney)	**STYLE:** Statue of a soldier on a column
BUILDER: UDC	**FABRICATOR:** Cordele Marble Co. (McKenney)

"YOUR SONS AND DAUGHTERS
WILL FOREVER GUARD
THE MEMORY OF YOUR
BRAVE DEEDS."

"IN MEMORIAM OUR HEROES
1861–1865,"

IT HAS NO SPEECH NOR LANGUAGE.
WITHIN ITS FOLDS THE
DEAD WHO DIED UNDER IT LIE
FITLY SHROUDED.

*(This inscription is placed below
crossed battle flags.)*

"FIDELITY, WHEN EXTENDED
TO HIM TO WHOM IT IS
JUSTLY DUE, RESEMBLES THE
"STARS OF FREIDLAND" THAT
SHINE BEST IN THE
BLACKEST NIGHT."

*(This is a quote from Evans, 10:282. The
reference is to the cavalry escorting Jefferson
Davis. This is in chapter 27, in the section of the
book covering Louisiana, written by John
Dimitry. Theodore A. Dimitry, a Louisiana
artilleryman, was among the bodyguard.)*

The monument cost $4,000 and is 35 feet high. It was erected in April 1909, but remained veiled for three years while the Oconee Chapter of the UDC tried to raise money to pay the fabricator. The monument was finally dedicated April 26, 1912 (McKenney).

The Confederate Veteran (29/8 [August 1921]) contains a McNeel advertisement that mentions a monument in Dublin that was under construction at the time. The Dublin monument was dedicated nine years earlier. There is no other monument in Dublin. The reference in the Confederate Veteran is a mystery. It may be that work was begun on a second Dublin monument but never finished.

A CSA monogram is inscribed on pediments above each side of the plinth. The dates of the war and crossed battle flags are repeated on the front and rear of the plinth. Other carvings include rifles crossed with a flag, crossed sabers, crossed cannon barrels and cannonballs, and another cannon barrel crossed with a rammer. Upright cannon barrels form pilasters at the corners of the plinth.

The soldier's pose is unusual. The rifle barrel is resting in the crook of his arm. He hands seem busy with some task; perhaps he is lighting a pipe like his comrade in Stewart County.

Liberty County, Hinesville

LOCATION: Courthouse grounds, facing South Commerce Street		
DATE: 1928	**STYLE:** Statue of a soldier on a pedestal	**BUILDER:** UDC

1861–1865

WAR BETWEEN THE STATES

ERECTED BY THE LIBERTY
COUNTY CHAPTER,
UNITED DAUGHTERS OF
THE CONFEDERACY,
IN MEMORY OF THE CON-
FEDERATE SOLDIERS OF
LIBERTY COUNTY,
THE RECORD OF WHOSE
SUBLIME SELF-SACRIFICE
AND UNDYING DEVOTION
TO DUTY IN THE SERVICE
OF THEIR COUNTRY IS
THE PROUD HERITAGE OF
A LOYAL POSTERITY.

C. S. A.

OUR
CONFEDERATE DEAD

LORD GOD OF HOSTS,
DEFEND US YET
LEST WE FORGET
LEST WE FORGET

*(From "Recessional" by Rudyard Kipling,
with a slight variation)*

LIBERTY VOLUNTEERS
CO. H 25TH REGT.
GA. INFANTRY

ALTAHAMA SCOUTS
CO. I 25TH REGT.
GA. INFANTRY

TROOP H
29TH BATT. GA.
CAVALRY

LIBERTY INDEPENDENT
TROOP G
5TH GA. CAVALRY

LIBERTY GUARDS
TROOP D 5TH GA.
CAVALRY

LIBERTY MOUNTED
RANGERS
JEFF DAVIS LEGION,
TROOP B 20TH BATT. GA.
CAVALRY

According to McKenney, this monument was the last soldier monument built in Georgia and is one of two "manifest cavalrymen" in the state. Jasper County's monument definitely has a statue of a cavalryman. Baldwin County's monument is less definite, but the soldier facing west does seem to be a cavalryman, so this Liberty County horse soldier is probably one of three, not one of two. Since McKenney's book was published, more soldier monuments have been added to the inventory.

Beneath the soldier is a Confederate Battle Flag. There are no other decorations or symbols.

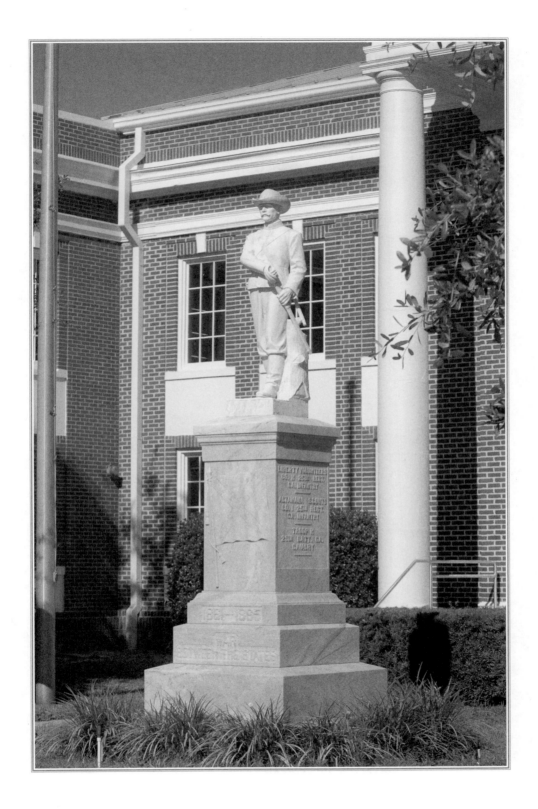

Lincoln County, Lincolnton

LOCATION: Traffic island on Washington Street, north of Main Street	
DATE: 1924 (McKenney)	**STYLE**: Memorial stone

TO THE MEMORY

OF THE

CONFEDERATE SOLDIERS

OF

LINCOLN COUNTY

Above the inscription are crossed flags, the First National and Third National, with "61–65" under the flags.

Lowndes County, Valdosta

LOCATION: Courthouse grounds, facing North Patterson Street and West Central Avenue		
DATE: 1911	**STYLE:** Statue of a soldier on a column	**BUILDER:** UDC
FABRICATOR: McNeel Marble Co. (McNeel Memorials)		

ERECTED BY
VALDOSTA CHAPTER,
U.D.C. No. 471.
1911.

"LEST WE FORGET."

COMRADES

OUR
CONFEDERATE
DEAD

THE PRINCIPLES FOR
WHICH THEY FOUGHT
LIVE ETERNALLY.

"CSA" is inscribed on the front and rear pediments above the plinth; the dates of the war are shown on the side pediments. Confederate Battle Flags on broken staffs are carved on two sides of the plinth.

Two large stone cannon balls rest on the base left and right of the plinth. The soldier is standing at rest.

The statue is made of Italian marble (UDC 2002).

GEORGIA'S CONFEDERATE MONUMENTS

Macon County, Montezuma

LOCATION: Fanny Carmichael Park, north of downtown Montezuma		
DATE: 1911	**BUILDER:** UDC	**STYLE:** Statue of a soldier on a column

NO NATION ROSE SO FAIR

AND WHITE

OR FELL SO PURE OF CRIME

(From "The Grand Old Bard" by Philip Stanhope Worsley, slightly misquoted)

ERECTED BY THE

PHIL COOK

CHAPTER

U.D.C.

JAN. 19, 1911

IN HONOR OF THE

CONFEDERATE

SOLDIERS

OF

MACON COUNTY

GEORGIA

GLORIA VICTIS

MACON COUNTY

HOLDS IN PROUD AND

GRATEFUL REMEMBRA-

NCE HER BRAVE AND

LOYAL SONS WHO

PREFERRED DEATH TO

BETRAYAL OF HER

PRINCIPLES.

The monument was moved to its current location in 1965 from the center of Dooly Street downtown (McKenney).

The front of the column is decorated with a Confederate Battle Flag. Two bronze lion heads protrude from the sides of the plinth. These are spouts for now-inoperable fountains. The soldier is standing at rest.

"C.S.A." is inscribed on all four sides at the top of the column; "1861–1865" appears on all four sides at the bottom.

Macon County, Oglethorpe

LOCATION: Courthouse grounds, South Sumter Street	**DATE:** 1924 (McKenney)
STYLE: Memorial stone	**BUILDER:** UDC

TO OUR
CONFEDERATE
DEAD

ERECTED BY
OGLETHORPE CHAPTER
NO 1407. U. D. C.
FEB. 20, 1923.

Although the monument bears the date 1923, the actual date of the dedication was April 26, 1924. The stone is Georgia granite. It was moved to the courthouse in 1935 from its original location at the junction of Georgia Highway 49 and Sumter Street. There was an artesian well at that location. The monument originally contained a fountain (McKenney).

Oglethorpe is the seat of Macon County. The monument in the nearby city of Montezuma predates the Oglethorpe monument by thirteen years. There were two UDC chapters in Macon County, the Oglethorpe Chapter, responsible for this monument, and the Phil Cook Chapter, which built the Montezuma monument. The older monument is dedicated to the Confederate soldiers of Macon County. The newer monument avoids redundancy with the dedication to "Our Confederate Dead."

"C.S.A." is inscribed on the front and back, above crossed flags. Crossed rifles decorate the front and rear at the bottom of the stone. A cannonball tops the monument. Urns are placed on the sides.

GEORGIA'S CONFEDERATE MONUMENTS

Madison County, Colbert

LOCATION: Georgia Highway 72 and South Fourth Street		DATE: 2003
STYLE: Obelisk	BUILDER: SCV	FABRICATOR: North Georgia Monument Co.

IN MEMORY OF
THE 400+ GALLANT
MADISON COUNTY
CONFEDERATES WHO
SACRIFICED SO MUCH FOR
SOUTHERN INDEPENDENCE

COMPANY "A"
16TH GEORGIA
VOLUNTEER INFANTRY
"THE MADISON COUNTY GREYS"
159 MEMBERS

COMPANY "D"
9TH GEORGIA
COMPANY "E"
36TH GEORGIA
COMPANY "C"
16TH GEORGIA
3RD GEORGIA
GUARD CAVALRY
COMPANY "G"
25TH BN. GEORGIA GUARD
MADISON COUNTY HOME
GUARD
AND OTHERS

COMPANY "D"
16TH GEORGIA
VOLUNTEER INFANTRY
"THE DANIELSVILLE GUARDS"
105 MEMBERS

ERECTED BY MADISON COUNTY
GREYS CAMP 1526
SONS OF CONFEDERATE
VETERANS 2003

THIS MEMORIAL DONATED BY
NORTH GEORGIA MONUMENT
CO CARLTON GA

Battle flags, in color, decorate all four sides above the inscriptions.

Marion County, Buena Vista

LOCATION: Courthouse grounds, facing McDuffie Street	DATE: 1916
STYLE: Memorial bench with a fountain in the center	
BUILDER: UDC and citizens of the Marion County	
FABRICATOR: McNeel Marble Co. (McNeel Memorials)	

ERECTED BY
MARION COUNTY CHAPTER
U.D.C.
AND CITIZENS, TO THE
CONFEDERATE SOLDIERS
OF THIS COUNTY.
JUNE 1916.

The inscription is carved on the tall upright behind the now-inoperable fountain. On the face in front of the reservoir are the dates of the war and a CSA monogram inside a wreath. Cannonballs, now missing, once rested on each end.

Marion County, Buena Vista

LOCATION: Courthouse grounds, facing Broad Street | **STYLE**: Memorial stone

THADDEUS OLIVER
POET AND CONFEDERATE
HERO

AUTHOR OF THE GREAT POEM
"ALL QUIET ALONG THE POTOMAC TONIGHT"

1826   1864

Thaddeus Oliver was a native of Jeffersonville, Georgia. He died of wounds in August 1864.

Authorship of the famous poem is disputed.

McDuffie County, Thomson

LOCATION: Courthouse grounds, Main Street	**DATE:** 1896
STYLE: Obelisk	**BUILDER:** LMA (CSMA, p. 159)

WOMANS TRIBUTE
APRIL 26, 1896.

CONFEDERATE DEAD

IN MEMORY OF
OUR FALLEN HEROES
OF McDUFFIE AND
COLUMBIA COUNTIES.

"THEY SLEEP THE SLEEP OF
OUR NOBLE SLAIN
DEFEATED, YET WITHOUT
A STAIN. PROUDLY AND
PEACEFULLY"

*(This is a slightly altered version of the final lines
of "The Sword of Robert Lee" by Abram J. Ryan.)*

This monument is unusual in that it honors the Confederate dead from two counties. Columbia County had previously placed a tablet inside its own courthouse. Decades later other monuments were erected in the county.

McDuffie County, Thomson

LOCATION: Main Street, between Railroad Street and Hendricks Street	
DATE: 1913 (McKenney)	**STYLE:** Statue of a woman in the center of a stone bench
BUILDERS: Veterans, UDC, and the Woman's Club of Thomson	
FABRICATOR: McNeel Marble Co. (McNeel Memorials)	

IN MEMORY OF

THE WOMEN

OF THE SIXTIES

AND THE

CONFEDERATE SOLDIERS

ERECTED

BY

THE VETERANS,

THE U.D.C.

AND

THE WOMAN'S CLUB

OF

THOMSON.

The stalwart woman is bearing a flag of uncertain design. A bowl at the base of the plinth appears to be the remnant of a fountain.

The statue is made of marble and was carved in Italy (Buzzett).

McIntosh County, Darien

LOCATION: Courthouse grounds, North Way	**DATE:** 1916
STYLE: Memorial fountain	**BUILDER:** UDC

1916

ERECTED IN MEMORY OF
THE MEN WHO WORE THE
GRAY 61–65
BY THE McINTOSH
CHAPTER U.D.C.

FOR THE COOL OF THE
WATERS THAT RUN
THROUGH THE SHADOWY
PLACES, I WILL GIVE THANKS
AND ADORE THEE, GOD
OF THE OPEN AIR.

(From "God of the Open Air" by Henry Van Dyke)

IN MEMORY
OF
MILLER COUNTY
CONFEDERATE
SOLDIERS AND
SAILORS THAT
HONORABLY
SERVED IN THE
WAR BETWEEN
THE STATES.
1861 – 1865

C
S
A

★ ★ CSA ★ ★

Miller County, Colquitt

LOCATION: Courthouse grounds, facing South First Street		
DATE: 2003	STYLE: Obelisk	BUILDER: SCV

IN MEMORY
OF
MILLER COUNTY
CONFEDERATE
SOLDIERS AND
SAILORS THAT
HONORABLY
SERVED IN THE
WAR BETWEEN
THE STATES.
1861–1865

NOT COMPREHEND.
THESE MEN ENDURED
COUNTLESS HARDSHIPS
FOR STATES RIGHTS
AND SOUTHERN
INDEPENDENCE. IT IS
FOR THESE REASONS
THAT WE HONOR OUR
ANCESTORS, LEST THE
COUNTRY FORGET
THEIR SACRIFICES.

WE HONOR OUR
CONFEDERATES FOR
THEIR COURAGE,
LOVE OF FAMILY,
AND DEDICATION TO
PRINCIPLES THAT MANY
IN TODAY'S WORLD CAN

ERECTED BY
SONS OF
CONFEDERATE VETERANS
DECATUR GRAYS
CAMP 1689
IN THE YEAR OF OUR LORD
2003

"CSA" and four stars are inscribed on the front of the base. The other sides of the base have three stars each. "CSA" is repeated in large, vertical letters on the left side. The SCV logo appears on the rear.

The monument was dedicated by David Hunter, a Real Son (Wiggins).

Mitchell County, Pelham

LOCATION: City Cemetery, Cemetery Road	**DATE:** 1938
STYLE: Stone and metal gateway	**BUILDER:** UDC

UDC MEMORIAL

DEDICATED
TO THE MEMORY
OF THE
CONFEDERATE VETERANS
OF
MITCHELL COUNTY
GEORGIA
1861–1865

ERECTED
BY THE
UNITED DAUGHTERS
OF THE
CONFEDERACY
PELHAM CHAPTER
APRIL 26, 1938

GEORGIA'S CONFEDERATE MONUMENTS

Monroe County, Forsyth

LOCATION: Courthouse grounds, West Johnston Street and North Lee Street	
DATE: 1908 (McKenney)	**STYLE:** Bronze statue on a pedestal
BUILDERS: Confederate Monument Association of Monroe County and the UDC (McKenney)	
FABRICATORS: Butler Marble and Granite Co. and the American Bronze Foundry Co. of Chicago (McKenney)	
SCULPTOR: Frederick C. Hibbard (McKenney)	

CONFEDERATE

GEORGIA VOLUNTEERS

QUITMAN GUARDS CO. K 1ST REG.

CONFEDERATE VOLUNTEERS CO. A 14TH REG.

MONROE CROWDERS CO. D 31ST REG.

MONROE VOLUNTEERS CO. H 32ND REG.

RUTLAND VOLUNTEERS CO. B 45TH REG.

McCOWEN GUARDS CO. D 45TH REG.

QUITMAN GUARDS CO. K 53RD REG.

A bronze tablet on the granite pedestal displays the Georgia Coat of Arms, flags of uncertain design, and the inscription. The cost of the monument was $3,000 (McKenney).

Montgomery County, Mount Vernon

LOCATION: Courthouse grounds, facing South Railroad Avenue	DATE: 1997
STYLE: Obelisk **BUILDER:** Friends and supporters of SCV	

DEDICATED TO THE GLORY AND
HONOR OF THE MONTGOMERY
COUNTY SOLDIERS OF THE
CONFEDERATE STATES OF AMERICA
FOR THEIR UNPARALLELED
COURAGE
AND GALLANTRY IN DEFENSE OF
THEIR
HOMELAND AND TO THEIR FAMILIES
AND
FRIENDS FOR THEIR SACRIFICES
AND UNWAVERING LOVE AND
SUPPORT.

ERECTED BY FRIENDS AND
SUPPORTERS OF
GENERAL ROBERT A. TOOMBS CAMP
932
SONS OF CONFEDERATE VETERANS
ERECTED 1997

1861 CONFEDERATE 1865

CONFEDERATE STATES

DECEMBER 1860
SOUTH CAROLINA

FEBRUARY 1861
MISSISSIPPI
FLORIDA
ALABAMA
GEORGIA
LOUISIANA
TEXAS

APRIL 1861
VIRGINIA
ARKANSAS
TENNESSEE
NORTH CAROLINA

PROVISIONAL
KENTUCKY
MISSOURI

OUR BOYS

THE CALL WENT OUT FROM
RICHMOND,
TO TOWNSHIPS GREAT AND SMALL.
OUR SOUTHERN LAND IS
THREATENED.
THE YANKEES TREAD OUR SOIL.
OUR BOYS ROSE UP
TO MEET THE FOE
AND PROTECT OUR DIXIELAND.
THEY FORCED THEM OUT OF
SUMTER,
THEN JACKSON MADE HIS STAND.

IN MANY DIFFERENT PLACES
OUR BOYS FOUGHT VALIANTLY,
IN SUMMER HEAT AND WINTER COLD,
WITH JOHNSTON, JACKSON, LEE.

THROUGH MANY BATTLES
WON AND LOST
OUR BOYS WERE PROUD AND BRAVE,
FOR HERITAGE AND SOUTHERN RIGHTS,
THEY GAVE THEIR ALL TO SAVE.

LEE MURDOCK

CSA

IT IS WELL THAT
WAR IS SO TERRIBLE,
ELSE MEN WOULD
LEARN TO LOVE IT
TOO MUCH.
ROBERT E. LEE
DO YOUR DUTY IN
ALL THINGS. YOU
CANNOT DO MORE.
YOU SHOULD NEVER
WISH TO DO LESS.

ROBERT. E. LEE

WELL, IF WE ARE TO
DIE, LET US DIE LIKE
MEN.
PAT CLEBURNE
FRANKLIN, TN
DEC. 1864

The date of the Cleburne quote is incorrect: he was killed at the Battle of Franklin on November 30. The second Lee quote is taken from a letter that was probably not written by Lee, although it was long accepted as authentic.

The Great Seal of the Confederacy and a Confederate Battle Flag decorate the front and rear of the obelisk.

Morgan County, Madison

LOCATION: Hill Park, South Main Street	**DATE:** 1909 (McKenney)
STYLE: Statue of a soldier on a column	**BUILDER:** UDC
FABRICATOR: McNeel Marble Co. (McNeel Memorials)	

"LORD GOD OF HOSTS,
BE WITH US YET,
LEST WE FORGET,
LEST WE FORGET."
(From "Recessional" by Rudyard Kipling)

"NO NATION ROSE
SO WHITE AND FAIR,
NONE FELL SO PURE
OF CRIME."
*(From "The Grand Old Bard" by Philip
Stanhope Worsley)*

1861–1865

TO THE SOLDIERS
OF THE
SOUTHERN CONFEDERACY
WHO DIED TO REPEL
UNCONSTITUTIONAL INVASION,

TO PROTECT THE RIGHTS
RESERVED TO THE PEOPLE,
TO PERPETUATE FOREVER
THE SOVEREIGNTY
OF THE STATES.
ERECTED BY THE
MORGAN COUNTY CHAPTER
OF THE UNITED
DAUGHTERS OF
THE CONFEDERACY,
1908.

"THEIR HEROISM ABIDES
IN OUR HEARTS.
THEIR UNCHALLENGED
DEVOTION AND MATCHLESS
VALOR SHALL CONTINUE
TO BE THE WONDER AND
INSPIRATION OF THE AGES."

The statue originally stood on the town square and was moved on an unknown date because of increasing traffic (McKenney).

A CSA monogram is set in wreath between the quotes from Kipling and Worsley. Crossed rifles are on one side of the column. On the other side is the Confederate Battle Flag on a broken staff.

The soldier is standing at rest.

Muscogee County, Columbus

LOCATION: In the median of Broadway, between West Seventh Street and West Eighth Street

DATE: 1879 | STYLE: Obelisk | BUILDER: LMA

FABRICATOR: Muldoon and Karnes of Louisville, Ky. (McKenney)

OUR CONFEDERATE DEAD.

IN MEMORIAM.

"NO TRUTH IS LOST FOR WHICH THE
TRUE ARE WEEPING NOR DEAD FOR
WHICH THEY DIED."

(From "Under the Willows"
by Francis O. Ticknor)

THEIR GLORY
SHALL
NOT BE FORGOTTEN

ERECTED
BY THE LADIES OF THE MEMORIAL
ASSOCIATION MAY, 1879,
TO HONOR THE
CONFEDERATE SOLDIERS
WHO DIED
TO REPEL UNCONSTITUTIONAL
INVASION, TO
PROTECT THE RIGHT RESERVED
TO THE PEOPLE, AND TO
PERPETUATE FOREVER THE
SOVEREIGNTY OF THE
STATES.

HONOR
TO THE BRAVE

"GATHER THE SACRED DUST,
OF WARRIORS TRIED AND TRUE,
WHO BORE THE FLAG OF OUR
NATIONS TRUST
AND FELL IN THE CAUSE THO' LOST,
STILL JUST
AND DIED FOR ME AND YOU."

(From "The March of the Deathless Dead"
by Abram J. Ryan)

The draped obelisk and the steps are made of marble. The steps were added to heighten the monument in 1881. The original cost was $4,500. The steps cost $500 (McKenney).

The obelisk is topped with an urn. The front is decorated with carvings of the Georgia Coat of Arms; a battle scene with a cannon, cannonballs, bayoneted rifles, sabers, drums, and bugles; and the Great Seal of the Confederacy.

Newton County, Covington

LOCATION: Town square, facing Monticello Street	DATE: 1906	
STYLE: Statue of a soldier on a pedestal		

BUILDER: According to McKenney, an ill-defined group identified variously at the time as the Ladies' Memorial Association, the United Daughters of the Confederacy, and the memorial committee was responsible for the monument.

FABRICATOR: Butler Marble and Granite Co. (McKenney)

TO THE CONFEDERATE DEAD
OF NEWTON COUNTY.

THEIR GALLANT AND HEROIC DEEDS
LIKE MONUMENTAL SHAFTS ARISE
FROM OUT THE GRAVEYARD
OF THE PAST
AND MARK THE TOMBS
WHERE VALOR LIES.

ERECTED APRIL 26, 1906

NO SORDID OR MERCENARY
SPIRIT ANIMATED THE
CAUSE ESPOUSED BY THOSE
TO WHOM THIS MONUMENT
IS ERECTED OR INSPIRED THE
MEN WHO BRAVELY FOUGHT
AND THE WOMEN WHO FREELY
SUFFERED FOR IT. ITS FINAL
FAILURE COULD NOT
DISHONOR IT NOR DID DEFEAT
ESTRANGE ITS DEVOTEES.

WHILE THIS MONUMENT
IS ERECTED IN MEMORY
OF CONFEDERATE SOLDIERS

AND THE SACRED CAUSE
FOR WHICH THEY CONTENDED
IT IS ALSO INTENDED TO
COMMEMORATE THE NOBLE
WOMEN WHOSE PEERLESS
PATRIOTISM AND SUBLIME
LIVES OF HEROIC AND
SELF-SACRIFICING SER-
VICE ENHANCED THE
HOLINESS OF THAT CAUSE
AND PROLONGED THE
STRUGGLE FOR ITS SU-
PREMACY BY INSPIRING
ITS CHAMPIONS WITH
INCREASED ARDOR ENTHU-
SIASM AND GALLANTRY
IN THE CONTEST.

ITS FAME ON BRIGHTEST PAGES,
PENNED BY POETS AND BY SAGES,
SHALL GO SOUNDING DOWN THE
AGES-FURL ITS FOLDS THOUGH
NOW WE MUST.

(From "The Conquered Banner"
by Abram J. Ryan.)

The statue is made of metal, though it is so similar in color to the stone base that its material is not readily apparent. The soldier is leaning backward, possibly because of structural damage.

Round pilasters are set in the corners of the plinth. The pediments above the plinth are decorated with crossed sabers, crossed cannon barrels, crossed rifles, and an anchor. Three sides of the plinth have inscriptions, the fourth displays the Confederate Battle Flag.

The soldier is standing at rest.

Newton County, Oxford

LOCATION: Cemetery on the campus of Oxford College of Emory University

DATE: 1872 (Widener)	STYLE: Obelisk

OUR

SOLDIERS

Oconee County, Watkinsville

LOCATION: Courthouse grounds, North Main Street	**DATE:** 1927 (McKenney)
STYLE: Memorial stone with a bronze tablet	**BUILDER:** UDC

ERECTED BY
ROBERTA HARRIS WELLS CHAPTER, U.D.C.
OF WATKINSVILLE
COMMEMORATING THE SELF-SACRIFICE
OF THE CONFEDERATE SOLDIER
WHOSE VALOR IS ENGRAVED UPON
THE HEART OF THE SOUTH,
ENDURING AS TIME, EXCITING
AND COMPELLING THE ADMIRATION
OF ALL NATIONS AND ALL PEOPLES

The monument was originally in City Park. It was moved to the courthouse grounds in the 1930s. After the courthouse burned in 1939 the monument was again moved and placed in front of the new courthouse (McKenney).

Oglethorpe County, Lexington

LOCATION: Courthouse grounds, Main Street	**DATE:** 1916
STYLE: Statue of a soldier on a rectangular base	**BUILDER:** UDC
FABRICATOR: McNeel Marble Co. (*Confederate Veteran*, 24/7 [July 1916])	

OUR CONFEDERATE SOLDIERS
1861–1865

"IN SIMPLE OBEDIENCE TO DUTY AS THEY
UNDERSTOOD IT, THESE MEN SUFFERED ALL,
SACRIFICED ALL, DARED ALL AND DIED."
M.S. WEAVER, COM. U.C.V. OF O.C.

ERECTED BY
OGLETHORPE CHAPTER
U.D.C.   1916.

"TO THE MEMORY OF THE MEN WHO
MET THE INEVITABLE AND
DIED FOR THINGS IMMORTAL."

The first quote ("In simple obedience..." etc.) appears to be attributed to M. S. Weaver, the commander of the United Confederate Veterans of Oglethorpe County. However, a longer version of the same quote is found on the Confederate memorial at Arlington National Cemetery. The words were written by Randolph Harrison McKim. The monument in downtown Wrightsville (Johnson County) also contains part of the McKim quote. The monument in Paulding County uses the entire passage. See the entry for Paulding County for more information.

The granite base lists the names of hundreds of local men in the Echols Artillery, three infantry companies—the Oglethorpe Rifles, the Tom Cobb Infantry, the Gilmer Blues (Company K, 6th Georgia)—and other, unnamed companies. The names cover the broad front and rear faces of the base and the narrow sides as well.

UDC 2002 contains all the names listed on the base. The names are the work of the WPA (Buzzett).

The monument is referenced in the McNeel advertisement on the back cover of the July 1916 issue of the Confederate Veteran.

The very young solder is standing at rest.

GEORGIA'S CONFEDERATE MONUMENTS

Paulding County, Dallas

LOCATION: Park on Hardee Street	**DATE:** 2012	**STYLE:** Statue of a soldier on a pedestal
BUILDER: SCV	**SCULPTOR:** Don Haugen	

1861–1865

LEST WE
FORGET

THE
CONFEDERATE
SOLDIER

PAULDING COUNTY

DEDICATED BY THE
GEN. WILLIAM J. HARDEE
CAMP # 1397.
SONS OF CONFEDERATE
VETERANS AND
PATRIOTIC CITIZENS WHO
GENEROUSLY CONTRIBUTED.

ERECTED IN 2012
DURING THE
SESQUICENTENNIAL OF THE
WAR BETWEEN THE STATES.

The final inscription is taken from the inscription on the Confederate memorial at Arlington National Cemetery, written by Randolph Harrison McKim, a Confederate veteran who, after the war, served as an Episcopal minister in Washington (Arlington National Cemetery's website, http://arlingtoncemetery.mil, accessed November 2011). Parts of the Arlington inscription are also found on the monument in Oglethorpe County and the Johnson County monument in downtown Wrightsville.

NOT FOR FAME OR REWARD
NOT FOR PLACE OR
FOR RANK
NOT LURED BY AMBITION
OR GOADED BY NECESSITY,
BUT IN SIMPLE OBEDIENCE
TO DUTY AS THEY
UNDERSTOOD IT, THESE
MEN SUFFERED ALL,
SACRIFICED ALL,
DARED ALL AND DIED.

The monument, commissioned by the SCV's General William J. Hardee Camp 1397, was dedicated on May 26, 2012. Real Daughter Iris Gay Jordan participated in the ceremony. Mrs. Jordan is the daughter of Lewis Gay, a corporal of the 4th Florida Infantry. The base is made of Georgia granite and was fabricated by Baston Monuments of Elberton. The cost of the monument was $43,000. (Conversations with Stevan Crew, June 2012).

The same artist sculpted the statue in Jefferson (Jackson County) dedicated eight months before this one.

A wreath is engraved on the front. On the rear are thirteen stars encircling the Georgia Coat of Arms. Above the coat of arms is "STATE OF GEORGIA" and below "IN GOD WE TRUST."

Peach County, Powersville

LOCATION: Cliett Cemetery, Georgia Highway 247 Connector and Barker Road

| DATE: 2002 | STYLE: Memorial wall | BUILDER: SCV |

THIS SITE DEDICATED TO THE
CONFEDERATE SOLDIERS OF GEORGIA
OF WHOM MANY PAID THE
ULTIMATE SACRIFICE
IN DEFENSE OF THEIR STATE
AND THEIR NATION, THE
CONFEDERATE STATES OF AMERICA
DURING THE WAR FOR
SOUTHERN INDEPENDENCE
1861–1865

"CARVED OUT OF THE
ENDURANCE OF
GRANITE, GOD CREATED
HIS MASTERPIECE—
THE CONFEDERATE SOLDIER."

—LILLIAN HENDERSON

DEDICATED
FEB. 23, 2002 BY THE
LT. JAMES T. WOODWARD
CAMP 1399, S.C.V.

NONE GREATER
NONE MORE HONORABLE

DEO VINDICE

This monument is one of three quoting Lillian Henderson, author of Roster of
Confederate Soldiers of Georgia 1861–1865. *The others are in Atkinson County and
Whitfield County (the memorial wall in Dalton's Confederate cemetery).*
The SCV logo is carved at the top of the center element of the wall.

GEORGIA'S CONFEDERATE MONUMENTS

Polk County, Cedartown

LOCATION: Courthouse grounds, facing Prior Street	**DATE:** 1906
STYLE: Statue of a soldier on a column	**BUILDER:** UDC
FABRICATOR: McNeel Marble Co. (McNeel Memorials)	

OUR HEROES

ERECTED BY THE
CEDARTOWN CHAPTER.
U.D.C. No. 491.
TO THE CONFEDERATE
VETERANS OF POLK COUNTY.
1906.

THE DAUGHTERS OF
THOSE WHO MADE
OUR FLAG, HOLD IN
EXALTED VENERATION
THOSE WHO BORE IT.

WHEN THE LAST
TRUMPET IS SOUNDED,
MAY EACH ONE ANSWER
THE ROLL CALL OF
THE HEAVENLY ARMY.
(Unknown source)

61,
THE PRINCIPLES FOR
WHICH THEY FOUGHT
LIVE ETERNALLY.
65.

THIS, WE RAISE, A
LOVING TRIBUTE TO
THE PAST, PRESENT
AND FUTURE.

*(The final quote is also found
on the Franklin County monument and
is from unidentified source.)*

Cannon barrels form pilasters at the corners of the plinth. The sides contain carvings of crossed flags, rifles, and sabers, and a CSA monogram. The soldier is standing at rest. The cost was $2,000 (McKenney).

Pulaski County, Hawkinsville

LOCATION: Courthouse grounds, Commerce Street

DATE: 1907 (McKenney) or 1908 (Widener)

STYLE: Statue of a soldier on a column with statues of Lee and Jackson at the base

BUILDER: Daughters of the Confederacy

FABRICATOR: McNeel Marble Co. (McNeel Memorials)

COMRADES

TO OUR

CONFEDERATE

SOLDIERS

ERECTED BY THE

DAUGHTERS OF THE CONFEDERACY

MRS. G.W. JORDAN, PRES.

MRS. P.H. LOVEJOY, SEC. AND TREAS.

The generals originally stood with their backs to the plinth. The change was made probably after an auto accident damaged the monument ca. 1935. The cost of the monument was $3,000. The original location was at an intersection in the center of town. The monument was moved to another intersection because of traffic, but the precaution was for naught, as the accident occurred at the second location. After this mishap the monument was moved to the courthouse. Jackson's arm was broken off in the accident and not repaired until 1981 (McKenney).

A battle flag with a broken staff decorates the front of the column; crossed rifles the rear. "1861–1865" is carved in pediments above the plinth on the sides. "CSA" is on the front and rear pediments. The private is standing at rest.

GEORGIA'S CONFEDERATE MONUMENTS

Putnam County, Eatonton

LOCATION: West Marion Street and South Madison Street, in front of the courthouse	
DATE: 1908 (McKenney)	**STYLE:** Statue of a soldier on a pedestal
BUILDERS: UDC and UCV	**FABRICATOR:** McNeel Marble Co. (McNeel Memorials)

A TRIBUTE OF LOVE
FROM THE DIXIE CHAPTER
DAUGHTERS OF
THE CONFEDERACY.
IN HONOR OF THE MEN
OF PUTNAM COUNTY,
WHO SERVED IN THE ARMY
OF THE CONFEDERATE
STATES OF AMERICA;
"THOSE WHO FOUGHT
AND LIVED, AND THOSE
WHO FOUGHT AND DIED."

"WHEN MARBLE WEARS AWAY,
AND MONUMENTS ARE DUST,
THE SONGS THAT GUARD
OUR SOLDIER'S CLAY,
WILL STILL FULFIL THEIR TRUST."
(From "Sentinel Songs" by Abram J. Ryan)

TO THE WOMEN OF THE SOUTHERN
CONFEDERACY.
WHOSE LOVING ADMINISTRATION
NURSED THE WOUNDED TO HEALTH,
AND SOOTHED THE LAST HOURS
OF THE DYING;
WHOSE UNSELFISH LABORS
SUPPLIED THE WANTS OF THEIR
DEFENDERS IN THE FIELD.
WHOSE UNWAVERING FAITH
IN OUR CAUSE
SHOWED EVER A GUIDING STAR;
THROUGH THE PERILS
AND DISASTERS OF WAR;
WHOSE SUBLIME FORTITUDE
SUSTAINED THEM UNDER EVERY
PRIVATION AND ALL SUFFERING:
WHOSE FLORAL OFFERINGS
ARE YEARLY LAID UPON THE GRAVES
OF THOSE
WHOM THEY STILL HONOR AND LOVE;
AND WHOSE PATRIOTISM
WILL TEACH THEIR CHILDREN
TO EMULATE
THE DEEDS OF THEIR
CONFEDERATE SIRES
BUT, WHO WITH A MODESTY EXCELLED
ONLY BY THEIR WORTH
HAVE EVER DISCOURAGED
THIS TRIBUTE TO THEIR NOBLE VIRTUES.

BY R.T. DAVIS. CAMP No. 759. U.C.V.

The statue is made of Italian marble; the base of granite. The cost was $1,900 (McKenney). One side of the pedestal has the Confederate Battle Flag and the dates of the war. "OUR CONFEDERATE DEAD" is inscribed on the base, with one word on each of three sides. On the fourth side is "LEST WE FORGET."

The soldier is standing at rest.

Rabun County, Clayton

LOCATION: Courthouse grounds, Courthouse Square and East Savannah Street		
DATE: 1999	STYLE: Memorial stone with a bronze tablet	BUILDER: UDC

WE HONOR WITH
AFFECTION, REVERENCE
AND UNDYING REMEMBRANCE
THOSE FROM RABUN COUNTY
WHO SERVED THE CONFEDERACY

1861–1865

ERECTED BY THE
MILDRED LEWIS RUTHERFORD
CHAPTER UDC 1999

WE HONOR WITH
AFFECTION, REVERENCE
AND UNDYING REMEMBRANCE
THOSE FROM RABUN COUNTY
WHO SERVED THE CONFEDERACY

1861 - 1865

ERECTED BY THE
MILDRED LEWIS RUTHERFORD
CHAPTER UDC 1999

GEORGIA'S CONFEDERATE MONUMENTS

Randolph County, Cuthbert

LOCATION: Town square, facing Pearl Street	**DATE:** 1896 (Widener) or 1898 (McKenney)
STYLE: Statue of a soldier on a round column	**BUILDERS:** UCV, LMA, and UDC

TO
OUR CONFEDERATE
DEAD.
1861. 1865.

ERECTED APRIL 26, 1896.
UNDER THE AUSPICES OF
RANDOLPH
CAMP No. 465. U.C.V. AND OF THE
LADIES MEMORIAL ASSOCIATION OF
RANDOLPH COUNTY.

THEY STRUGGLED FOR
CONSTITUTIONAL GOVERNMENT
AS ESTABLISHED BY OUR FATHERS
AND THOUGH DEFEATED, THEY LEFT
TO POSTERITY A RECORD OF HONOR
AND GLORY MORE VALUABLE THAN
POWER OR RICHES.

HEROISM AND LOVE OF
COUNTRY WERE NEVER MORE
GRANDLY ILLUSTRATED THAN
UPON THE FIELDS WHERE

CONFEDERATE SOLDIERS FOUGHT
AND DIED. LET FUTURE
GENERATIONS HONOR AND
EMULATE THEIR VIRTUES.

THOUGH OVERPOWERED
THEIR CAUSE WAS NOT LOST, FOR
"EACH SINGLE WRECK IN
THE WARPATH OF MIGHT
SHALL YET BE A ROCK IN
THE TEMPLE OF RIGHT."
(From "A Land without Ruins"
by Abram J. Ryan)

LET THE GLORIOUS
RECORD OF OUR SOLDIERS
AND THE SACRED CAUSE
FOR WHICH THEY FOUGHT
BE KEPT EVER FRESH AND
GREEN IN MEMORY'S WASTE.

A tornado toppled the statue in 1909 and damaged the soldier. A new one was erected and the damaged statue placed in Greenwood Cemetery. The new statue, carved in Italy, was erected in 1910. The Stonewall Jackson Chapter of the UDC was responsible for the new statue (McKenney).

The soldier has an unusual pose: he is holding his rifle with his right hand, with his left hand held over his eyes as if to shield them from the sun. Four round pilasters are set in the corners of the plinth. At the bottom of the column, above the plinth, are crossed rifles, sabers, cannon barrels, and an anchor.

Richmond County, Augusta

LOCATION: In the median of Broad Street, between Seventh Street and Eighth Street	
DATE: 1878	**STYLE:** Statue of a soldier on a tall column, with four statues at the base
BUILDER: LMA	
DESIGNERS: Van Gunden and Young of Philadelphia (CSMA, p. 109; McKenney)	

IN MEMORIAM

"NO NATION ROSE WHO WHITE

AND FAIR:

NONE FELL SO PURE OF CRIME."

(From "The Grand Old Bard" by Philip Stanhope Worsley)

ERECTED
A.D. 1878.
BY
THE LADIES
MEMORIAL ASSOCIATION
OF AUGUSTA.
IN HONOR OF THE MEN OF
RICHMOND COUNTY.
WHO DIED
IN THE CAUSE OF THE
CONFEDERATE STATES.

WORTHY
TO HAVE LIVED AND KNOWN
OUR GRATITUDE:
WORTHY
TO BE HALLOWED AND HELD
IN TENDER REMEMBRANCE:

WORTHY
THE FADELESS FAME WHICH
CONFEDERATE SOLDIERS
WON.
WHO GAVE THEMSELVES IN LIFE
AND DEATH FOR US:
FOR THE HONOR OF GEORGIA.
FOR THE RIGHTS OF THE STATES.
FOR THE LIBERTIES OF THE PEOPLE.
FOR THE SENTIMENTS OF THE
SOUTH.
FOR THE PRINCIPLES OF THE
UNION.
AS THESE WERE HANDED DOWN TO
THEM BY THE FATHERS OF
OUR COMMON COUNTRY.

The monument contains a carving of a symbol very similar to the state's coat of arms. On one surface of the base is a symbol similar to the Great Seal of the Confederacy. Behind this symbol are rifles, cannonballs, a flag, a drum, and a bugle.

There is also a carving of the Second National Flag (with an unusually long fly), draped on its staff, and crossed with saber and rifle. A third carving shows two flags (which appear to be US flags) beneath a wreath and draped over crossed cannon barrels.

Berry Benson, a local veteran, was the model for the statue, posing for a photograph used by the Italian sculptor. The monument is dedicated to the Confederate dead of Richmond County.

The monument's cost was over $17,000. The shaft is made of Carrara marble. The base is Georgia granite. Seventy-six feet in height, the monument is the tallest in the state. Stonewall Jackson's widow was present at the dedication. The monument was erected by Theodore Markwalter (CSMA, p. 109; McKenney).

McKenney names the designer VanGunder and Young. In CSMA, it is Van Gunden and Young.

At the base of the monument are statues of generals Robert E. Lee, Stonewall Jackson, W. H. T. Walker, and T. R. R. Cobb.

Richmond County, Augusta

LOCATION: In the median of Greene Street, between Fourth Street and Fifth Street	
DATE: 1873 (McKenney)	**STYLE:** Obelisk
BUILDERS: The Cenotaph Club and St. James' Sabbath School	**FABRICATOR:** Markwalter

DULCE ET DECORUM EST
PRO PATRIA MORI.

IMMORTALIS EST
VERITAS.

THESE MEN DIED
IN DEFENCE OF
THE PRINCIPLES
OF THE
DECLARATION OF
INDEPENDENCE

MARKWALTER
AUGUSTA GA.

BY THE CENOTAPH CLUB
TO THE "BOYS IN GRAY" FROM
AUGUSTA AND RICHMOND COUNTY.

ST. JAMES' SABBATH SCHOOL
DEDICATES THIS TABLET
TO HER FALLEN HEROES.

Three sides of the plinth contain tablets listing the county's dead. The tablet honoring the fallen Sabbath School members contains twenty-four names. On the other tablets, the names are so numerous that they do not fit entirely on the tablets and spill over to the base beneath. The dead are listed according to their rank, with Major General W. H. T. Walker topping the list.

UDC 2002 lists all the names engraved on the cenotaph. Crossed flags, crossed rifles, and a wreath are carved on the shaft.

The obelisk is made of marble.

Richmond County, Augusta

LOCATION: Walton Way and Aumond Road	**DATE:** 1926
STYLE: Boulder with two flat surfaces for the inscriptions	
BUILDER: Annie Wheeler Auxiliary 3 USWV	

JOSEPH WHEELER

BORN ON THIS SITE, SEPT. 10 1836

LT. GEN. COM. CONFEDERATE CAVALRY 1865

MAJ. GEN. COM. U. S. CAVALRY 1898

"HIS NAME AND FAME WILL LIVE AND BE LOVED AS LONG

AS NOBLE DEEDS ARE HONORED AMONG MEN"

PLACED BY

ANNIE WHEELER AUXILIARY NO. 3. U.S.W.V.

1926

"THE LORD SHALL COUNT WHEN

HE WRITETH UP HIS PEOPLE, THAT

THIS MAN WAS BORN THERE."

PSALM 87-6

Above the main inscription are crossed United States and Confederate flags. Joseph Wheeler was one of the four young Confederate generals who, more than thirty years after the Civil War, were commissioned as generals in the United States Army during the Spanish-American War.

GEORGIA'S CONFEDERATE MONUMENTS

Richmond County, Augusta

LOCATION: Goodrich Street, between the Augusta Canal and the Savannah River

DATE: 1872 (Date the structure was dedicated as a Confederate memorial, according to Wiggins)

STYLE: Chimney, built as part of the Confederate Powder Works

THIS
OBELISK-CHIMNEY,
SOLE REMNANT OF THE EXTENSIVE
POWDER-WORKS HERE ERECTED
UNDER THE AUSPICES OF THE
CONFEDERATE GOVERNMENT,
IS, BY THE CONFEDERATE
SURVIVORS ASSOCIATION
OF AUGUSTA, WITH THE CONSENT
OF THE CITY COUNCIL, CONSERVED
IN HONOR OF A FALLEN NATION,
AND INSCRIBED TO THE MEMORY
OF THOSE WHO DIED IN THE
SOUTHERN ARMIES DURING
THE WAR BETWEEN THE STATES.

GEORGE WASHINGTON RAINS
U. S. M. A.
BRIGADIER-GENERAL-ORDNANCE, C. S. A.
BREVET-MAJOR, U. S. A.
CAPTAIN. 4TH ARTILLERY.
WHO UNDER ALMOST INSUPERABLE
DIFFICULTIES ERECTED,
AND SUCCESSFULLY OPERATED
THESE POWDER-WORKS –
A BULWARK OF THE BELEAGUERED
CONFEDERACY.

The construction of the powder works, of which the chimney was a part, was completed in April 1862. Ten years later the United States government deeded the property to the city of Augusta. At the request of Colonel Rains, the chimney was kept as a memorial.

A battle flag made of metal is affixed to the chimney below the first inscription.

Stone tablets with these two inscriptions are set in the brick chimney. A marker erected in 2003 by Georgia Civil War Heritage Trails is at the base of the chimney and tells more fully the story of the powder works.

Richmond County, Augusta

LOCATION: Magnolia Cemetery, Third Street	**DATE:** 1994
STYLE: Bronze tablet on a brick base	**BUILDER:** SCV

THIS MEMORIAL IS DEDICATED TO THE MEMORY OF
THESE 7 BRAVE SOLDIERS WHO REST ELSEWHERE IN
MAGNOLIA. THEY FOUGHT AGAINST OPPRESSION,
TYRANNY, ABSOLUTE POWER AND USURPATION OF
STATES' RIGHTS, ALL OF WHICH STILL PLAGUE OUR
COUNTRY. ERECTED BY E. PORTER ALEXANDER CAMP
158, SONS OF CONFEDERATE VETERANS.

COMMANDER WOODY HIGHSMITH   ADJUTANT WALKER McWEE
LT. CMDR. TONY CARR   JUDGE ADV. K.C. WATSON

THIS 15 DAY OF JANUARY 1994.

Seven headstones, set in a brick and gravel bed, form an arc above the tablet.

Richmond County, Augusta

LOCATION: In the median of Greene Street, between Seventh Street and Eighth Street		
DATE: 1913	**STYLE:** Stone block housed in a portico	**BUILDER:** Anna Russell Cole

Father Abram Joseph Ryan is known as the poet-priest of the South. His works are quoted on Georgia's monuments more often than any other writer's works. He lived in Augusta between 1868 and 1870.

James Ryder Randall was, like Ryan, a native of Maryland and a staunch Confederate. After the war, he was a writer and editor for the Augusta Chronicle. He died in Augusta in 1908.

Paul Hamilton Hayne was a poet, magazine editor, and literary critic. A native of Charleston, he moved to Grovetown, Georgia, near Augusta, when Charleston was bombarded in 1862. Grovetown was his home until his death in 1888.

Sidney Lanier was a Confederate veteran, teacher, lawyer, musician, and Georgia's most famous poet. He served as a pilot for blockade runners and was captured. He died at age thirty-nine of tuberculosis, which he contracted during his imprisonment at Point Lookout, Maryland.

The stone block is housed inside a portico with four Doric columns.

FATHER RYAN
1839–1886

TO THE HIGHER SHRINE OF LOVE DIVINE
MY LOWLY FEET HAVE TROD,
I WANT NO FAME, NO OTHER NAME
THAN THIS—A PRIEST OF GOD!

(Ryan wrote these words, his own epitaph, shortly before his death in 1886.)

SIDNEY LANIER
1842–1881

THE CATHOLIC MAN WHO HATH MIGHTILY WON
GOD OUT OF KNOWLEDGE AND GOOD OUT OF INFINITE PAIN
AND SIGHT OUT OF BLINDNESS AND PURITY OUTOF A STAIN.

(From "The Marshes of Glynn")

JAMES R. RANDALL
1839–1908

BETTER THE FIRE UPON THEE ROLL,
BETTER THE BLADE, THE SHOT, THE BOWL,
THAN CRUCIFIXION OF THE SOUL,
MARYLAND! MY MARYLAND!

(From "Maryland, My Maryland")

PAUL HAYNE
1830–1888

YET WOULD I RATHER IN THE OUTWARD STATE
OF SONG'S IMMORTAL TEMPLE LAY ME DOWN,
A BEGGAR BASKING BY THAT RADIANT GATE
THAN BEND BENEATH THE HAUGHTIEST EMPIRE'S
CROWN!

(From "The Will and the Wing")

TO THE CITY OF AUGUSTA
ANNA RUSSELL COLE
1913

Richmond County, Fort Gordon

LOCATION: Cemetery 30, Gibson Road and Jones Chapel Road	
STYLE: Stone column	**BUILDER:** Linwood Sunday School

ERECTED

TO THE MEMORY

OF

OUR BOYS IN GRAY

BY THE

LINWOOD

SUNDAY SCHOOL.

JUNE—1866

This is Georgia's earliest Confederate monument. The twenty-three names inscribed on this modest memorial show the ghastly cost of the war for this one country church and for the nation.

Rockdale County, Conyers

LOCATION: South Main Street and Court Street	DATE: 1913
STYLE: Statue of a soldier on a column	BUILDER: UDC
FABRICATOR: McNeel Marble Co. (McNeel Memorials)	

TO THE
CONFEDERATE
VETERANS
OF ROCKDALE COUNTY.

MANY OF WHOM
GAVE ALL,
ALL OF WHOM
GAVE MUCH.

ERECTED BY THE
CONYERS CHAPTER
OF THE
UNITED DAUGHTERS
OF THE CONFEDERACY,
1913.

On the front of the plinth, below "1861–1865," a Confederate Battle Flag is crossed with the Third National. Stone cannonballs are set at the corners.

The monument was dedicated on Confederate Memorial Day, 1913 (McKenney).

The soldier is standing at rest.

Schley County, Ellaville

LOCATION: Park in the center of town, facing West Oglethorpe Street		
DATE: 1910	STYLE: Statue of a soldier on a column	BUILDER: UDC

IN MEMORY OF
THE
BOYS IN GRAY

ERECTED 1910
UNDER THE AUSPICES
OF THE
SARAH E. HORNADY
CHAPTER
U. D. C.

YEA – AND WHEN
THRONES SHALL
CRUMBLE DOWN
AND HUMAN
PRIDE AND
GRANDEUR FALL –
PERISHING
GLORIES ALL –
THE PURE
DEVOTION OF
THY VALIANT
HEART
SHALL LIVE IN
HEAVEN OF WHICH
IT IS A PART.

(From "The Female Martyr"
by John Greenleaf Whittier)

"SONS OF THE CHOICEST
STRAIN OF AMERICAN
BLOOD, SCIONS OF REVOLUTION-
ARY STOCK, CITIZENS
OF THE PUREST SECTION
OF THIS UNION THEY
LIVED TRUE TO EVERY
HONORABLE TRADITION
THAT ILLUMINATES THE
PAGES OF OUR HISTORY
AND AT THE CALL OF DUTY
LAID DOWN THEIR LIVES A
NOBLE SACRIFICE ON THE
ALTAR OF THEIR COUNTRY.

(Unknown source)

TELL IT AS
YOU MAY
IT NEVER
CAN BE TOLD
THE STORY
OF THE GLORY
OF THE MEN
WHO WORE
THE GRAY

(From "The Men Who Wore the Gray"
by Abram J. Ryan)

The Confederate Battle Flag graces the front of the column. "1861–1865" appears below the flag. "CSA" is inscribed on all four sides of the column, just beneath the soldier. There are inoperable fountains at the base in front and rear. The soldier is standing at rest.

The monument originally stood at Oglethorpe and Broad streets (McKenney). The park is at that same intersection.

The monument was moved to the park in 1937 (Americus Times-Recorder, March 15, 2010, quoting Margaret Goodwin).

Screven County, Sylvania

LOCATION: Screven County Memorial Cemetery, East Ogeechee Street

DATE: 1909 | **STYLE:** Statue of a soldier on a column

BUILDERS: UDC and the sons of veterans
(As the inscription says merely "SONS OF VETERANS," and mentions no specific camp,
the reference may not be to SCV as an organization.)

FABRICATOR: McNeel Marble Co. (McNeel Memorials)

TO THE CONFEDERATE SOL-
DIERS WHO WENT FROM SCREVEN
COUNTY TO FIGHT FOR THE SOUTH
IN THE WAR BETWEEN THE STATES,
AND WHO FROM 1861 TO '65 NOBLY
ILLUSTRATED GEORGIA ON THE
FIELD OF BATTLE, THIS MONU-
MENT IS ERECTED BY THEIR
DESCENDANTS AS A MEMORIAL
OF THEIR DEEDS.

CONFEDERATE
DEAD

"NO NATION ROSE SO WHITE
AND FAIR,
OR FELL SO PURE OF CRIME."
*(From "The Grand Old Bard" by Philip
Stanhope Worsley, slightly misquoted)*

WHEN THE CALL CAME THEY
LEFT ALL FOR THE FRONT,
AND FOR FOUR YEARS, WITH-
OUT RECOMPENSE OR REWARD,
THEY FOUGHT BRAVELY FOR
LOCAL SELF GOVERNMENT
AND THE RIGHTS OF THE
STATES.

ERECTED BY THE
SCREVEN COUNTY CHAP-
TER OF THE UNITED
DAUGHTERS OF THE
CONFEDERACY AND THE
SONS OF VETERANS,
APRIL 26, A. D. 1909.

The monument was moved to Memorial Cemetery ca. 1950 when its original location, a downtown park, was made into a parking lot (McKenney). The author is in possession of a postcard showing the monument at its original location.

There are four stone cannonballs on the corners of the base. The soldier is standing at rest. There are no symbols carved on any of the monument's surfaces.

Both the column and the statue are marble.

Spalding County, Griffin

LOCATION: Park at East Taylor Street and First Street, containing several war monuments			
DATE: 1909	**STYLE:** Statue of a soldier on a column		**BUILDER:** UDC
FABRICATOR: McNeel Marble Co. (McNeel Memorials)			

ERECTED BY
JAMES BOYNTON CHAPTER
UNITED DAUGHTERS
OF THE CONFEDERACY,
OF GRIFFIN
AND SPALDING COUNTY,
NOVEMBER, 1909.

THEIR MAUSOLEUM
IS OUR HEART,
THEIR FAME HATH
DEATHLESS BLOOM;
TIME IS THEIR
WATCHFUL SENTINEL,
AND GLORY GUARDS
THEIR TOMB.

OUR TRIBUTE OF
GRATITUDE, REVERENCE,
AND LOVE TO THE SOLDIERS,
OF THE CONFEDERATE
STATES OF AMERICA.
1861–1865

IN EVERLASTING
REMEMBRANCE OF THE
HEROIC DEEDS, SUBLIME
SELF-SACRIFICE
AND UNDYING DEVOTION
TO DUTY AND COUNTRY,
OF SPALDING COUNTY'S
CONFEDERATE SOLDIERS.

The column is decorated with crossed rifles, a CSA monogram in a wreath, and the Great Seal of the Confederacy. There is also a Confederate Battle Flag partially furled on a broken staff. The soldier is standing at rest.

The monument was originally at Hill and Solomon streets, and was moved to the park in the 1970s (McKenney).

Spalding County, Griffin

LOCATION: Stonewall Cemetery, East Taylor Street		**DATE:** 1869
STYLE: Statue of an angel on a pedestal		
BUILDER: LMA	**FABRICATOR:** G.B. Rooks	**SCULPTOR:** S. F. Oatman, Atlanta

IN MEMORIAM.

OUR
CONFEDERATE
DEAD

ERECTED
BY THE
LADIES MEMORIAL
ASSOCIATION
OF GRIFFIN, GA.
1869.

REST! SOLDIERS! REST!

The following inscription is largely indecipherable, but enough words are legible to indicate that it is "An Ode Written at the Beginning of the Year 1746" by William Taylor Collins.

HOW SLEEP THE BRAVE,
WHO SINK TO REST
BY ALL THEIR COUNTRY'S WISHES BLEST!
WHEN SPRING,
WITH DEWY FINGERS COLD,
RETURNS TO DECK
THEIR HALLOW'D MOULD,
SHE THERE SHALL DRESS
A SWEETER SOD
THAN FANCY'S FEET HAVE EVER TROD.

BY FAIRY HANDS THEIR KNELL IS RUNG;
BY FORMS UNSEEN THEIR DIRGE IS SUNG;
THERE HONOUR COMES,
A PILGRIM'S GREY,
TO BLESS THE TURF THAT
WRAPS THEIR CLAY;
AND FREEDOM SHALL AWHILE REPAIR
TO DWELL, A WEEPING HERMIT, THERE!

According to U.D.C. 2002, citing A History of Griffin 1840-1940 *by Quimby Melton, Jr. (Hometown Press, Griffin, no date given), Rooks was a local contractor who made the base. The statue was the product of the Atlanta Marble Works. U.D.C. 2002 also states that S.F. Oatman and William Gray of the Atlanta Marble Works erected the angel and the shaft. It seems that Oatman, as he is credited on the monument itself, was the artist, not just one of the men responsible for construction.*

The statue cost $1,930 and was originally made for a private grave in Columbus. Another $1,900 was spent for the base (McKenney).

"S. F. OATMAN ATLANTA" is inscribed at the bottom of the upper element of the structure.

Spalding County, Griffin

LOCATION: Stonewall Cemetery, East Taylor Street	DATE: 1922
STYLE: Memorial stone with a bronze tablet	BUILDER: UDC

TO
THE WOMEN OF GRIFFIN
AND SPALDING COUNTY
WHO GAVE THEIR SERVICES
DURING THE WAR BETWEEN
THE STATES FROM '61 TO '65

JAMES S. BOYNTON CHAPTER
UNITED DAUGHTERS OF THE
CONFEDERACY HAVE PLACED
THIS BOULDER

NO ACT OF INJUSTICE, NO FAILURE
OF DUTY, NO SHADOW OF WRONG
HAS LEFT A BLOT UPON THESE SOULS
OR A STAIN UPON THEIR MEMORIES

A. D. 1922

Stephens County, Toccoa

LOCATION: Courthouse grounds, facing North Sage Street	**DATE**: 1922
STYLE: Obelisk	**BUILDER**: UDC

TO THE MEMORY

OF OUR

CONFEDERATE

DEAD

1861–1865

ERECTED BY TOCCOA CHAPTER

UNITED DAUGHTERS

OF THE CONFEDERACY

1922

SING IT AS YOU

WILL, IT NEVER

CAN BE SUNG,

TELL IT AS YOU

MAY, IT NEVER

CAN BE TOLD,

ALL THE GLORY

OF THE STORY OF

THE MEN, WHO

WORE THE GRAY.

*(From "The Men Who Wore the Gray"
by Abram J. Ryan with some alterations)*

A battle flag is carved on the outward side of the obelisk. The shaft and the plinth are made of marble.

Stewart County, Lumpkin

LOCATION: Courthouse grounds, West Broad Street	DATE: 1908
STYLE: Statue of a soldier on a column	BUILDER: UDC
FABRICATOR: McNeel Marble Co. (McNeel Memorials)	

IN MEMORY OF THE BRAVE
CONFEDERATE SOLDIERS
OF STEWART COUNTY
BOTH THOSE WHO FOUGHT
AND FELL, AND THOSE WHO
FOUGHT AND SURVIVED.

OUR SOLDIERS

ERECTED BY STEWART
COUNTY CHAPTER U. D. C.
AS A TRIBUTE OF LOVE
AND HONOR.

1908.

The pediments above the plinth are inscribed with the dates of the war, two with "1861" and two with "1865." "CSA" appears on each of the four pediments immediately below the statue. Three stars appear below each of these pediments. The front of the column contains crossed rifles, the rear a torn battle flag on a broken staff.

The soldier depicted here is one of the more casual Confederate heroes, as he calmly tamps tobacco in his pipe, with his rifle propped against his front.

GEORGIA'S CONFEDERATE MONUMENTS

Sumter County, Americus

LOCATION: Rees Park, facing Elm Avenue	DATE: 1899 (CSMA, p. 88)
STYLE: Statue of a soldier on a pedestal	BUILDERS: UDC and LMA (McKenney)

OUR
CONFEDERATE
DEAD
1861–1865.

TO THE MEMORY
OF THE
SOLDIERS
OF
SUMTER COUNTY
WHO DIED IN DEFENSE OF
THEIR COUNTRY

TO
THOSE WHO FOUGHT
IN THEIR RAGGED
OLD SUITS OF GRAY.

A CSA monogram appears beneath the soldier. The first two inscriptions quoted are set in shield-shaped cartouches on the sides of the plinth. The third is carved on the base. The soldier is in the charge bayonet position.

The monument's cost was $1,800 (CSMA, p. 88).

The original location was at Lee and Forsyth streets. The monument was moved to Rees Park after World War II (McKenney).

The monument had deteriorated over the years and was further damaged in a 2004 hurricane. It was restored by the local SCV camp (Wiggins).

The rifle and bayonet are made of metal.

Sumter County, Andersonville

LOCATION: Church Street and Oglethorpe Street

DATE: 1908 (www.exploresouthernhistory.com, accessed December 2011) or 1909 (UDC 2002)

STYLE: Obelisk | BUILDER: UDC

IN MEMORY
CAPTAIN HENRY WIRZ.
C.S.A.
BORN ZURICH, SWITZERLAND,
1822
SENTENCED TO DEATH
AND EXECUTED AT
WASHINGTON, D. C.
NOV. 10, 1865.

TO RESCUE HIS NAME FROM
THE STIGMA
ATTACHED TO IT BY
EMBITTERED PREJUDICE,
THIS SHAFT IS ERECTED BY
THE GEORGIA DIVISION
UNITED DAUGHTERS OF THE
CONFEDERACY.

WIRZ

DISCHARGING HIS DUTY WITH
SUCH HUMANITY
AS THE HARSH
CIRCUMSTANCES OF THE TIMES
AND THE POLICY OF THE FOE
PERMITTED,
CAPTAIN WIRZ BECAME AT LAST
THE VICTIM
OF A MISDIRECTED
POPULAR CLAMOR.

HE WAS ARRESTED IN TIME
OF PEACE,
WHILE UNDER THE PROTECTION
OF A PAROLE,
TRIED BY A MILITARY
COMMISSION
OF A SERVICE TO WHICH
HE DID NOT BELONG
AND CONDEMNED TO
IGNOMINIOUS DEATH
ON CHARGES OF EXCESSIVE
CRUELTY
TO FEDERAL PRISONERS.
HE INDIGNANTLY SPURNED
A PARDON,
PROFFERRED ON CONDITION
THAT HE WOULD INCRIMINATE
PRESIDENT DAVIS
AND THUS EXONERATE
HIMSELF FROM
CHARGES OF WHICH BOTH
WERE INNOCENT.

WHEN TIME SHALL
HAVE SOFTENED
PASSION AND PREJUDICE
WHEN REASON SHALL HAVE
STRIPPED THE
MASK FROM
MISREPRESENTATION
THEN JUSTICE HOLDING

EVENLY HER SCALES
WILL REQUIRE MUCH OF PAST
CENSURE
AND PRAISE TO CHANGE
PLACES.
JEFFERSON DAVIS,
DEC. 1888.

IT IS HARD ON OUR MEN HELD IN
SOUTHERN
PRISONS NOT TO EXCHANGE
THEM
BUT IT IS HUMANITY
TO THOSE LEFT IN THE RANKS
TO FIGHT OUR BATTLES.
AT THIS PARTICULAR TIME TO
RELEASE ALL REBEL
PRISONERS NORTH
WOULD INSURE SHERMAN'S
DEFEAT
AND WOULD COMPROMISE OUR
SAFETY HERE
ULYSSES S. GRANT,
AUG. 18, 1864.

Talbot County, Talbotton

LOCATION: Courthouse grounds, facing Washington Avenue		
DATE: 1904	STYLE: Obelisk	BUILDER: UDC

1861–1865.

OUR CONFEDERATE
HEROES

ERECTED BY THE
ALICE BEALL MATHEWS
CHAPTER U.D.C. 1904.

The front of the obelisk contains a partly furled battle flag on an unbroken staff. A CSA monogram inside a wreath is carved beneath the flag. The flag has an unusual feature, a cross tinted with blue. The cemetery monument in Newnan (Coweta County) is the only one other monument in Georgia with this characteristic.

Taliaferro County, Crawfordville

LOCATION: Courthouse grounds, Broad Street	**DATE:** 1898
STYLE: Obelisk	**BUILDER:** LMA (McKenney)

1861–1865.
ERECTED TO THE
MEMORY OF OUR
CONFEDERATE
DEAD,
APR. 26, 1898.

This simple obelisk, bearing no other inscriptions or carvings, stands on the walkway leading to the courthouse entrance.

The cost of the monument was $1,500. The dedication was held on April 30, not on Confederate Memorial Day as stated on the monument. The monument was originally sited in the road in front of the courthouse. In the 1930s, when the road was paved, it was relocated (McKenney). Monument Street, on the side of the courthouse, may have been the original location.

Taliaferro County, Crawfordville

LOCATION: On the grounds of Liberty Hall, facing Lexington Street

DATE: 1893 | STYLE: Statue of Alexander Hamilton Stephens

BORN FEB. 11, 1812,
MEMBER GA. HOUSE OF
REPRESENTATIVES,
1836 TO 1840,
MEMBER GA. STATE SENATE 1842,
MEMBER U.S. HOUSE OF
REPRESENTATIVES,
1843 TO 1859,
RETIRED FROM CONGRESS 1859,
VICE PRESIDENT CONFEDERATE STATES,
1861 TO 1865,
U.S. SENATOR ELECT FROM GEORGIA, 1866,
MEMBER U.S. HOUSE OF
REPRESENTATIVES,
1873 TO 1882.
GOVERNOR OF GEORGIA 1882,
DIED IN ATLANTA. GA,
SUNDAY MORNING MARCH 4, 1883.

AUTHOR OF "A CONSTITUTIONAL VIEW OF
THE WAR
BETWEEN THE STATES" AND OF A
COMPENDIUM OF
THE HISTORY OF THE UNITED STATES
FROM THEIR
EARLIEST SETTLEMENT TO 1872.

ALEXANDER H. STEPHENS

"I AM AFRAID OF NOTHING ON EARTH,
OR ABOVE THE EARTH, OR UNDER THE
EARTH, EXCEPT TO DO WRONG—THE
PATH OF DUTY I SHALL EVER ENDEAVOR
TO TRAVEL, 'FEARING NO EVIL' AND
DREADING NO CONSEQUENCES."

"HERE SLEEP THE REMAINS OF ONE WHO
DARED TO TELL THE PEOPLE THEY WERE
WRONG WHEN HE BELIEVED SO, AND WHO
NEVER INTENTIONALLY DECEIVED A
FRIEND OR BETRAYED EVEN AN ENEMY."

EXTRACTS FROM AUGUSTA SPEECH, 1855.

(This last quote is puzzling. It seems to be a description of Stephens, yet it is attributed to a speech that he himself made.)

THE GREAT COMMONER,
THE DEFENDER OF
CIVIL AND RELIGIOUS LIBERTY.
"HE COVETED AND TOOK FROM THE
REPUBLIC NOTHING SAVE GLORY."

The statue is next to Stephens' tomb in front of his home, Liberty Hall. Carved below the front of the statue is a wreath.

NON SIBI, SED ALIIS.

ERECTED 1893.

THROUGHOUT LIFE A SUFFERER IN BODY,
MIND, AND SPIRIT, HE WAS A SIGNAL
EXEMPLAR OF WISDOM, COURAGE,
FORTITUDE,
PATIENCE, AND UNWEARYING CHARITY,
IN THE DECREPITUDE OF AGE, CALLED TO
BE GOVERNOR OF THE STATE. HE DIED,
WHILE IN PERFORMANCE OF THE WORK
OF HIS OFFICE, AND IT SEEMED FIT,
THAT HAVING SURVIVED PARENTS,
BRETHREN, SISTERS, AND MOST OF
THE DEAR COMPANIONS OF YOUTH,
HE SHOULD LAY HIS DYING HEAD
UPON THE BOSOM OF HIS PEOPLE.

Taylor County, Butler

LOCATION: Courthouse grounds, facing Main Street	**DATE:** 1911
STYLE: Statue of a soldier on a column	**BUILDER:** UDC
FABRICATOR: National Marble & Granite Co. of Marietta (UDC 2002, citing the *Butler Herald*)	

IN HONOR
OF THE
BOYS IN GRAY
FROM
TAYLOR COUNTY

ERECTED BY THE
WALLACE EDWARDS
CHAPTER U. D. C.

OUR HEROES

NO NATION ROSE SO
PURE AND FAIR
OR FELL SO FREE OF
CRIME.

(From "The Grand Old Bard"
by Philip Stanhope Worsley, slightly altered)

The dates of the war are shown three times, twice on the plinth and once on the base. A battle flag on a broken staff is carved on the front of the column.

The soldier is standing at rest.

GEORGIA'S CONFEDERATE MONUMENTS

Terrell County, Dawson

LOCATION: Cedar Hill Cemetery, Stonewall Street	**DATE:** 1923
STYLE: Memorial stone	**BUILDER:** UDC

ERECTED BY
MARY BRANTLEY
CHAPTER, U. D. C.
TO MARK THE LAST RESTING PLACE
OF THE SLAVES WHO DIED DURING THE
WAR BETWEEN THE STATES
IN HUMBLE SERVICE, THEY WERE
FAITHFUL TO EVERY TRUST
FEBRUARY 1923

Thomas County, Thomasville

LOCATION: Courthouse grounds, facing Washington Street	**DATE**: 1879	
STYLE: Draped obelisk	**BUILDER**: LMA	
FABRICATOR: Muldoon Monument Co. (McKenney)		

ERECTED
BY THE LADIES
MEMORIAL ASSOCIATION.
1879.

IN MEMORY OF
THE
CONFEDERATE SOLDIERS.
OF THOMAS CO. GEO.
WHO DIED
DURING THE WAR 1861–5.

"ON FAME'S ETERNAL CAMPING GROUND
THEIR SILENT TENTS ARE SPREAD.
AND GLORY GUARDS WITH SOLEMN ROUND
THE BIVOUAC OF THE DEAD."
(From "The Bivouac of the Dead" by Theodore O'Hara)

The cost of the monument was $1,735. It was moved from its original location at Broad and Fletcher (now Remington) streets, ca. 1946, because of traffic (McKenney).

JUDGEMENT
1879

Thomas County, Thomasville

| LOCATION: Laurel Hill Cemetery, East Jackson Street | DATE: 1879 | STYLE: Statue |

JUDGEMENT
1879

This statue, "Judgement," was originally a part of the Forsyth Park monument in Savannah. It became superfluous when the Savannah monument was redesigned. See the entry for Savannah (Chatham County).

The statue was moved to Thomasville in 1879. The donation was arranged by Mrs. C. P. Hansell, a resident of Thomasville originally from Savannah (Wiggins).

According to the information on a headstone behind the statue, this small section of the cemetery is designated "Soldier's Circle." A captain, a corporal, and eleven privates are buried here.

Tift County, Tifton

LOCATION: Fulwood Park, Tift Avenue North and East 12th Street		**DATE:** 1910
STYLE: Statue of a soldier on a column		**BUILDER:** UDC
FABRICATOR: McNeel Marble Co. (McNeel Memorials)		

"LEST WE

FORGET."

(This quote from "Recessional" by Rudyard Kipling is encircled by a wreath, set in a cartouche, on the front of the plinth.)

CONFEDERATE

ERECTED BY THE

CHARLOTTE CARSON

CHAPTER OF THE

UNITED DAUGHTERS

OF THE CONFEDERACY

UNVEILED

APRIL 26TH 1910

TIFTON GA.

DEDICATED TO OUR

LIVING AND DEAD

CONFEDERATE SOLDIERS

1861–1865

This monument has had five homes, and is probably the most traveled monument in the state. It was originally at Love Avenue and Fourth Street; in the early 1940s it was moved to the courthouse; then to the center of Tift Avenue and 12th Street; then to Fulwood Park in 1975; and in 1992 to its new location in Fulwood Park, where it is now standing. The original cost was $2,000 (McKenney).

The soldier is standing at rest. A small metal tag on the base tells that the monument was relocated to this place on March 31, 1992.

"CSA" is inscribed in a diamond-shaped inset on the column just below the statue.

Toombs County, Vidalia

LOCATION: McMillan Burial Ground, Church Street	DATE: 1996
STYLE: Memorial stone	BUILDERS: SCV and UDC

THE SOUTHERN DEAD

THE SOUTHERN DEAD ARE SLEEPING
IN A THOUSAND SOUTHERN GLENS...
THE MOSS AND WILLOWS BECKON
WITH THE BREATH OF SOUTHERN WINDS.

THOUGH THE BLOOD-STAINED CROSS OF ST. ANDREW
IS TATTERED NOW AND FURLED...
THEY BORE IT HIGH ON EVERY FIELD
AND O'ER EVERY OCEAN OF THE WORLD.

IT WASN'T THROUGH THEIR FAILING
THAT THE GLEAMING TURNED TO RUST...
AND THE DREAMING OF A NATION
IS ENSHRINED WITHIN THEIR DUST.

SOME WOULD HAVE THEIR DEEDS FORGOT,
THEIR MONUMENTS SWEPT AWAY...
BUT WHILE SOUTHERN BLOOD FLOWS IN OUR VEINS,
THOSE KNAVES SHALL NEVER SEE THE DAY.

TEACH YOUR CHILDREN OF THEIR STORY
OF BATTLES, LOST AND WON...
THEY MUST KEEP MEMORY'S LIGHT A-BURNING
TILL SOUTHERN RIVERS CEASE TO RUN.

THE SOUTHERN DEAD ARE SLEEPING.
SGT. BENJ. R. GORMLEY

TO COMMEMORATE THE 100TH ANNIVERSARY
OF THE SONS OF CONFEDERATE VETERANS
1896–1996

DEDICATED BY THE SONS AND DAUGHTERS
OF THE CONFEDERACY, AND THE RE-ENACTORS
WHO STRIVE TO PRESERVE ITS SPIRIT

ERECTED BY THE GEN. ROBERT A. TOOMBS
CAMP. 932, SCV
CHAPTER 1329, UDC
DEO VINDICE

A Maltese cross with a wreath is engraved on the front. On the rear is a Confederate Battle Flag.

Troup County, LaGrange

LOCATION: Triangle at New Franklin Road and Franklin Street	DATE: 1902
STYLE: Statue of a soldier on a column	BUILDER: UDC

ERECTED BY THE UNITED
DAUGHTERS OF THE CONFED-
ERACY TO THE MEMORY OF
OUR CONFEDERATE SOLDIERS.
THOSE WHO FOUGHT AND DIED
AND THOSE WHO FOUGHT AND
LIVED.

OUR CONFEDERATE DEAD

"IN OUR HEARTS THEY PERISH NOT"

LEST WE FORGET.

(A metal tablet at the base reads:)
UNVEILED OCT. 30, 1902 BY
LOCAL CHAPTER OF U.D.C.

MOVED FROM COURTSQUARE IN 1943
TO GROUNDS OF NEW COURTHOUSE
ON RIDLEY AVE.

MOVED TO TRIANGLE ON
FRANKLIN RD. OCT. 16, 1976

PRESENTED BY HOLLY GARDEN CLUB—1980

Crossed sabers, "CSA," and the dates of the war are on the front of the column. A battle flag is on one side. The soldier is standing at rest.

Troup County, West Point

LOCATION: Fort Tyler Historic Site, Sixth Avenue	**DATE:** 1901 (McKenney)
STYLE: Obelisk	**BUILDERS:** UDC and LMA (McKenney)
	FABRICATOR: Ellidge & Nerman Co. (McKenney)

MORE ENDURING THAN MARBLE
SHALL BE THE MEMORY OF THE
CONFEDERATE PATRIOT IN WHOSE
LIFE FIDELITY TO PRINCIPLE FOUND
LOFTIEST EXPRESSION.

A TRIBUTE OF LOVE FROM
THE WOMEN OF THE SOUTH
TO THE HEROES OF THE
CONFEDERACY.

The inscription was written by Frank L. Stanton, the state's poet laureate. The monument was originally at the intersection of Ferry and Richmond, and later moved to a site at the river (McKenney).

The current location at Fort Tyler is the memorial's third home.

A battle flag, with its staff crossing a sword, is on one side of the shaft. On the opposite side is a wreath surrounding crossed rifles and a saber.

Turner County, Ashburn

LOCATION: Park at East Madison Avenue and Posey Lane | STYLE: Memorial stone

IN MEMORIAM.

OUR

CONFEDERATE AND WORLD WAR

HEROES

1861–65.　　1917-18.

This marker was formerly in Sycamore. It was moved to Ashburn sometime between 2002 and 2006. (The old location is pictured in U.D.C. 2002 and the new site is pictured in Wiggins.)

Twiggs County, Jeffersonville

LOCATION: US Highway 80 and South Ash Street	DATE: 1911
STYLE: Statue of a soldier on a column	BUILDER: UDC

TO THE TWIGGS COUNTY
SOLDIERS
AND THOSE WHO
SACRIFICED ALL
TO ESTABLISH THE
INDEPENDENCE OF
THE SOUTH
1861–1865

IN MEMORY

ERECTED
A. D. 1911
BY THE
TWIGGS COUNTY CHAPTER
DAUGHTERS OF THE
CONFEDERACY

FAULK INVINCIBLES
CAPT. E. S. GRIFFIN
26TH. GA. REG.

SLAPPEY GUARDS
CAPT. U. A. RICE
48TH. GA. REG.

TWIGGS VOLUNTEERS
CAPT. JAS. FOLSOM
4TH. GA. REG.

TWIGGS GUARDS
CAPT. JNO. BARCLAY
6TH. GA. REG.

This monument is unusual in that it names the captains of the companies listed on the monument. It is not uncommon for monuments to honor specifically the locally raised companies, but the names of individuals are rarely included.

A battle flag adorns the front of the column. The soldier is standing at rest. Most of the rifle is missing from the statue.

Union County, Blairsville

LOCATION: Veteran's Park on School Street	**DATE**: 1995	**STYLE**: Memorial stone
BUILDER: War Memorial Committee		
SCULPTOR: Gregory Johnson (Johnson's website, www.gregoryjohnson.biz, accessed July 2012)		

CIVIL WAR

The Civil War memorial is one element in a plaza of memorial stones honoring the Union County veterans of all wars. This is one of two memorials that honor Georgians who served in the Union forces. (The other is in nearby Gilmer County.)

On top of the stone block a bronze sculpture in mid-relief depicts two soldiers on picket duty or in some similar activity.

Beneath "CONFEDERATE ARMY" are the names of ninety-two Union County men who fought for the South. There are three names under "UNION ARMY."

GEORGIA'S CONFEDERATE MONUMENTS

Upson County, Thomaston

LOCATION: Courthouse grounds, facing Center Street	**DATE:** 1908
STYLE: Statue of a soldier on a column	**BUILDER:** UDC
FABRICATOR: McNeel Marble Co. (McKenney)	

IN MEMORY OF
THE CONFEDERATE
SOLDIERS OF UPSON.

OUR SOLDIERS

"LEST WE FORGET."

ERECTED. 1908.

On the pediments above the plinth, "1861" is inscribed on the front and rear and "1865" on the sides. The front of the column has a torn battle flag on a broken staff. One side has crossed rifles. "CSA" is inscribed on the front pediment at the top of the column. Stars surround the top of the column.

The cost of the monument was $1,300 (McKenney).

Some of the surfaces seem to have been prepared for additional inscriptions but were left blank. The soldier is standing at rest.

Upson County, Thomaston

LOCATION: Courthouse grounds, facing Center Street and Gordon Street | DATE: 1953

STYLE: Stone pedestal topped with a very special cannonball

FIRST CANNON BALL FIRED
AT OUTBREAK OF THE WAR
BETWEEN THE STATES, AT
FORT SUMTER, APRIL 12, 1861.

PRESENTED TO U.D.C. BY MRS.
SALLIE WHITE TO WHOM IT WAS
GIVEN IN 1861 BY P. W. ALEXANDER,
LEADING CONFEDERATE WAR
CORRESPONDENT, WHO WAS
PRESENT WHEN THE BALL WAS
FIRED, AND KNEW IT TO BE THE FIRST.

THE FIRST MARKER SUPPORTING
THIS BALL, STATING THESE FACTS,
WAS ERECTED ON THIS SQUARE IN 1919.

The new pedestal for the unique artifact was made in 1953 (Widener). UDC 2002 contains a photograph of the cannon ball on the original base.

Under the cannon ball is the Great Seal of the Confederacy.

FIRST CANNON BALL FIRED
AT OUTBREAK OF THE WAR
BETWEEN THE STATES, AT
FORT SUMTER, APRIL 12, 1861

PRESENTED TO U.D.C. BY MRS.
SALLIE WHITE TO WHOM IT WAS
GIVEN IN 1861 BY A.W. ALEXANDER,
LEADING CONFEDERATE WAR
CORRESPONDENT, WHO WAS
PRESENT WHEN THE BALL WAS
FIRED AND KNEW IT TO BE THE
FIRST.

THE FIRST MARKER SUPPORTING
THIS BALL, STATING THESE FACTS,
WAS ERECTED ON THIS SQUARE
IN 1919.

Upson County, Thomaston

LOCATION: Courthouse grounds, facing Center Street	**DATE**: 1938
STYLE: Sundial on a pedestal	**BUILDER**: UDC

GENERAL
JOHN B. GORDON

BORN
UPSON COUNTY
FEB. 6, 1832
DIED
JAN. 9, 1904

SOLDIER
OF THE
CONFEDERACY
STATESMAN
AND
CHRISTIAN GENTLEMAN

ERECTED
BY U.D.C.
1938

Walker County, Chickamauga

LOCATION: Chickamauga City Cemetery, facing West Seventh Street

DATE: 2005	STYLE: Memorial wall	BUILDER: SCV

"LEST WE FORGET..."

THIS MONUMENT IS DEDICATED TO THE CONFEDERATE
SOLDIERS LAID HERE TO REST IN THEIR BELOVED SOUTHERN
SOIL. THEY SACRIFICED SO THAT WE MAY ENDURE.

IN MEMORY OF JORDAN CHRISTOPHER LEE BOOHER
JAN. 6, 1994—JUNE 23, 2002

SONS OF CONFEDERATE VETERANS
JOHN INGRAHAM CAMP 1977
CHICKAMAUGA, GA—AD 2005

* * * * *

"WERE THESE THINGS REAL?
DID I SEE THOSE BRAVE AND NOBLE COUNTRY MEN OF MINE
LAID LOW IN DEATH AND WELTERING IN THEIR BLOOD?
DID I SEE OUR COUNTRY LAID WASTE AND IN RUINS?
DID I SEE SOLDIERS MARCHING, THE EARTH TREMBLING
AND JARRING BENEATH THEIR MEASURED TREAD?
DID I SEE THE RUINS OF SMOLDERING CITIES AND DESERTED HOMES?
DID I SEE THE FLAG OF MY COUNTRY, THAT I HAD FOLLOWED SO LONG,
FURLED TO BE NO MORE UNFURLED FOREVER?
SURELY THEY ARE BUT THE VAGARIES OF MINE OWN IMAGINATION....
BUT, HUSH! I NOW HEAR THE APPROACH OF BATTLE. THAT LOW,
RUMBLING SOUND IN THE WEST IS THEROAR OF CANNON IN THE DISTANCE."

PVT. SAM WATKINS
COMPANY AYTCH
1ST TENNESSEE

Above this quote from Company Aytch *is an image of crossed flags*
and battlefield debris. A scroll bears the following inscription:

"THE HANDS THAT GRASPED THEM,
AND THE HEARTS THAT FINALLY CLASPED THEM,
COLD AND DEAD ARE LYING LOW."

(A slightly altered quote from "The Conquered Banner" by Abram J. Ryan)

*On the center panel is an image of a battlefield grave,
with an inscription above and below.*

PVT. JOHN INGRAHAM
CAMP 1977

INGRAHAM GRAVE ON
CHICKAMAUGA BATTLEFIELD

CHICKAMAUGA, GEORGIA

The monument names the Confederate veterans buried in this cemetery. On the day the author visited, battle flags adorned the graves of most of the veterans. Some of the names—Brotherton, Dyer, Mullis—are familiar to anyone who has studied the Battle of Chickamauga.

The center panel of the wall contains the Great Seal of the Confederacy, the SCV logo and a battle scene showing Confederate riflemen fighting under a Confederate Battle Flag and beside a fallen comrade.

On the side panels are the names of forty-seven men who served in the Army of Tennessee and nineteen who served in the Army of Northern Virginia.

On the rear of the monument, the side panels display four Confederate flags—the Bonnie Blue, and the First, Second, and Third National.

Walker County, LaFayette

LOCATION: North Main Street, in front of the Chattooga Academy	**DATE**: 1909
STYLE: Statue of a soldier on a column	**BUILDER**: UDC
FABRICATOR: McNeel Marble Co. (McNeel Memorials)	

ERECTED 1909.
BY THE
CHICKAMAUGA CHAPTER OF
THE UNITED DAUGHTERS
OF THE CONFEDERACY,
TO THE
CONFEDERATE SOLDIERS,
OF WALKER COUNTY.

CONFEDERATE

TO OUR
CONFEDERATE
SOLDIERS.

"IT IS A DUTY WE OWE
TO POSTERITY, TO SEE
THAT OUR CHILDREN
SHALL KNOW THE VIRTUES,
AND BECOME WORTHY
OF THEIR SIRES."

(Jefferson Davis, from 1882 speech in New Orleans, with slight alteration [Sedore, p. 91])

"MANY OF WHOM GAVE ALL,
ALL OF WHOM GAVE MUCH."

"TO THOSE WHO WERE,
AND TO THOSE THAT ARE."

"CENTURIES
ON CENTURIES
SHALL GO
CIRCLING BY,
BUT THEY
ARE NOT DEAD,
THEIR MEMORIES
CAN NEVER DIE."

In 1968, the monument was moved from its original location in LaFayette Park, in the middle of town, to its present site (McKenney).

When the monument was moved, the Chattooga Academy building housed the chamber of commerce. Now it is used as a museum. An unsightly metal building close to the statue was removed and the grounds were transformed into an attractive park.

The statue is similar to the one in Perry (Houston County), also by McNeel, and is not typical of the company's work.

"CSA" is inscribed on the side pediments above the plinth. The inscription "1861–1865" is on the front and rear pediments. Crossed rifles are on one side of the plinth, a Confederate Battle Flag on the other.

The soldier is standing at rest.

Walker County, LaFayette

LOCATION: North Main Street, on the grounds of the Chattooga Academy		
DATE: 2002 (Wiggins)	STYLE: Memorial wall	BUILDER: SCV

COMPANIES AND REGIMENTS

OF

THE ARMY OF NORTHERN

VIRGINIA

AND

THE ARMY OF TENNESSEE

THAT THE MEN OF

WALKER COUNTY, GEORGIA

SERVED IN

*One side of the center panel depicts
a Confederate Battle Flag and
the above inscription.*

* * * * *

*The other side of the center panel contains the
Great Seal of the Confederacy, and the SCV and
UDC logos. On the same panel there are
inscriptions dedicating the monument and
crediting the builders.*

DEDICATED TO THE SOLDIERS

AND FAMILIES

OF WALKER COUNTY, GEORGIA

FOR THEIR SERVICE TO THE

CONFEDERATE STATES OF

AMERICA

1861–1865

"LEST WE FORGET"

JOHN B. GORDON

CAMP 599

CHICKAMAUGA

CHAPTER 1091

ERECTED BY

THE GEORGIA DIVISION

SONS OF CONFEDERATE

VETERANS

JOHN B. GORDON CAMP 599

LAFAYETTE, GEORGIA

OCT. 2001

*The four side panels are filled, on both sides, with the name of approximately 900 men.
Although the Chickamauga Chapter of the UDC is named on the monument, the
inscription specifically states that it was erected by the SCV.*

*Following this inscriptions are names of 109 units. "IN MEMORIAM OF
JONATHAN MAXEY" is inscribed below the names of the units.*

Walton County, Monroe

LOCATION: Courthouse grounds, facing Broad Street	**DATE:** 1907
STYLE: Statue of a soldier on a column	**BUILDERS:** LMA and surviving veterans
FABRICATOR: McNeel Marble Co. (McNeel Memorials)	

"ON FAME'S ETERNAL
CAMPING GROUND,
THEIR SILENT TENTS
ARE SPREAD,
AND GLORY GUARDS,
WITH SOLEMN ROUND,
THE BIVOUAC OF THE DEAD."

(From "The Bivouac of the Dead" by Theodore O'Hara)

COMRADES

TO OUR
CONFEDERATE
DEAD

"HOW SLEEP THE BRAVE,
WHO SINK TO REST,
BY ALL THEIR COUNTRY'S
WISHES BLEST."

(From "An Ode Written in the Beginning of the Year 1746" by Williams Collins)

ERECTED JUNE 1, 1907
BY THE LADIES MEMORIAL
ASSOCIATION AND SURVIVING
CONFEDERATE VETERANS.

"CSA" is inscribed on the front and rear pediments above the plinth; "1861–1865" on the side pediments. Crossed rifles are on one side of the column; crossed flags of uncertain design are on the other side, draped on their staffs.

The cost was $2,500 (McKenney).

Walton County, Monroe

LOCATION: West Haven Cemetery, East Spring Street

STYLE: Statue of Matthew Nunnally at his grave | **BUILDER:** Mary Nunnally Sandidge

NUNNALLY

ITS FAME ON BRIGHTEST PAGES
PENNED BY POETS AND BY SAGES
SHALL GO SOUNDING DOWN THE AGES
FURL ITS FOLDS THOUGH NOW WE MUST.

(From "The Conquered Banner" by Abram J. Ryan)

A TRIBUTE OF LOVING
REMEMBRANCE FROM
MARY NUNNALLY SANDIDGE
TO THE MEMORY
OF HER BROTHER,
WHOSE YOUNG
CAREER WAS BRIEF,
BRAVE AND GLORIOUS

The statue stands on a short column above the plinth. The letter "N" is carved on the pediment above the plinth below the front of the statue. On one surface of the plinth is a flag, draped on an unbroken staff, above the quote from "The Conquered Banner." Pilasters with Corinthian capitals are set in the corners of the plinth. Other inscriptions describe Nunnally's high character, his distinguished military service, and his death at Gettysburg.

GEORGIA'S CONFEDERATE MONUMENTS

Ware County, Waycross

LOCATION: Phoenix Park, Pendleton Street and Mary Street		
DATE: 1910 (McNeel Memorials)	**STYLE:** Statue of a soldier on a column	
BUILDER: UDC	**FABRICATOR:** McNeel Marble Co. (McNeel Memorials)	

1861–1865

CONFEDERATE
DEAD

ERECTED BY THE
FRANCIS S. BARTOW
CHAPTER U. D. C.
TO THE
CONFEDERATE
VETERANS.

ETERNAL RIGHT THOUGH
ALL THINGS FAIL, CAN
NEVER BE MADE WRONG.

"MANY OF WHOM GAVE
ALL, AND ALL OF WHOM
GAVE MUCH."

THE IMPARTIAL ENLIGHTENED
VERDICT OF MANKIND WILL
VINDICATE THE RECTITUDE
OF OUR CONDUCT,
AND HE WHO KNOWS THE
HEARTS OF MEN, WILL JUDGE
THE SINCERITY WITH WHICH
WE HAVE LABORED TO PRESERVE
THE GOVERNMENT OF OUR
FATHERS IN ITS SPIRIT.

JEFFERSON DAVIS.

The solder is on the march with his rifle on his right shoulder. Crossed battle flags are engraved on the front beneath the dates of the war. The monument is made entirely of marble.

Warren County, Warrenton

LOCATION: Courthouse grounds, Main Street	DATE: 1904 (Widener) or 1905 (McKenney)
STYLE: Statue of soldier on a column	BUILDER: The Matron's Club (Wiggins)
FABRICATOR: McNeel Marble Co. (McNeel Memorials)	

OUR

COMRADES

    This monument is short on verbiage and long on decoration. Carvings include crossed rifles on the front of the column, crossed sabers on the front of the base, cannon barrels serving as pilasters on the corners of the plinth, and a flag partly furled on its staff.

    "CSA" is engraved in a cartouche just below the rifles. The soldier is standing at rest.

    A granite slab in front of the monument contains a list of approximately 280 names of Warren County men who served in the forces of the Confederacy. UDC 2002 lists all the names that are still legible.

    The cost of this monument was $1,500 (McKenney).

Washington County, Sandersville

| LOCATION: City Cemetery, West Church Street | DATE: 1897 (McKenney) | STYLE: Obelisk |

TO THE MEMORY
OF THE
CONFEDERATE
SOLDIERS,
WHO ILLUSTRATED
WASHINGTON CO.,
ON MANY BATTLEFIELDS.
A HERO'S CROWN IS
THINE FOREVER.
THERE ARE DEEDS WHICH
SHOULD NOT PASS AWAY
AND NAMES THAT CANNOT
BE FORGOTTEN.
1861–1865.

C. S. A.

There is a CSA monogram in a cartouche above the plinth.

Washington County, Tennille

LOCATION: Park on North Main Street		DATE: 1917	STYLE: Fountain
BUILDER: UDC	FABRICATOR: Schneider Marble Company of Americus (McKenney)		

IN HONOR OF

OUR

CONFEDERATE

SOLDIERS

1861–1865

ERECTED

BY THE

JAMES D.

FRANKLIN

CHAPTER,

U.D.C.

1917

"CSA" and the St. Andrew's cross, with thirteen stars, are inscribed on all four sides of the column.

The monument cost $550 and was originally in the town square. The top of the shaft once held a white globe (McKenney).

The stone stands on each side of the fountain once held cannon barrels. They were there in 1994 and are shown in a photograph taken by the author at that time. The photograph shown here was taken in 2011.

The inscription on the monument reads:

ERECTED BY THE LADIES
MEMORIAL ASSOCIATION
OF WHITFIELD COUNTY
TO THE MEMORY OF
OUR CONFEDERATE DEAD
1892

Whitfield County, Dalton

LOCATION: Confederate Cemetery (West Hill Cemetery)	**DATE:** 1892
STYLE: Statue of a soldier on a pedestal	**BUILDER:** LMA
FABRICATOR: Muldoon Monument Co. (McKenney)	

ERECTED BY THE LADIES
MEMORIAL ASSOCIATION
OF WHITFIELD COUNTY,
TO THE MEMORY OF
OUR CONFEDERATE DEAD.
1892.

CONFEDERATE MEMORIAL

Names of nearby battles listed at base:
DALTON
ROCKY FACE
CHICKAMAUGA
RESACA

The marble statue was carved in Italy. The base also is of marble. The monument was originally located in a downtown park and was moved in 1971. The original cost was $2,000. The monument may have been erected in 1898, not the date on the monument. If that was the case, late payment to the contractor might have been the cause (McKenney).

The usual stump behind the statue is replaced here by a cannon barrel. The soldier is standing at rest.

A CSA monogram is engraved on the front. There is also a wreath on top of crossed sabers.

Whitfield County, Dalton

LOCATION: North Hamilton Street and West Crawford Street	**DATE:** 1912
STYLE: Bronze statue on a pedestal	**BUILDER:** UDC
SCULPTOR: Belle Kinney (*Dalton Daily Citizen*, October 7, 2012)	
FABRICATOR: Tiffany Studios cast the statue.	

JOSEPH E. JOHNSTON

1807–1891

BRIGADIER GENERAL U. S. A.

GENERAL C.S.A.

GIVEN COMMAND OF THE CONFEDERATE
FORCES AT DALTON, IN
1863, HE DIRECTED THE 79 DAYS
CAMPAIGN TO ATLANTA, ONE OF THE
MOST MEMORABLE IN THE ANNALS OF WAR

ERECTED BY BRYAN M. THOMAS
CHAPTER UNITED DAUGHTERS OF
CONFEDERACY DALTON, GEORGIA, 1912

At the base of the statue, in the rear:
CAST BY TIFFANY-STVDIOS, N.Y.

One cannot help but notice the very odd inscription. Johnston himself recognized that it was not he, but Sherman, who directed this campaign. The monument was restored and rededicated on October 20, 2012.

A Maltese cross inside a wreath is carved between the statue and the inscription.

Whitfield County, Dalton

LOCATION: Confederate Cemetery (West Hill Cemetery)		**DATE:** 1999
STYLE: Memorial wall	**BUILDERS:** The Civil War Round Table of Dalton, SCV, UDC	

GEN. JOSEPH E. JOHNSTON

CAMP #671

SONS OF CONFEDERATE VETERANS

PVT DREWRY R SMITH CHAPTER

UNITED DAUGHTERS OF THE CONFEDERACY

THE CIVIL WAR ROUND TABLE OF DALTON, INC.

"HISTORY PRESERVED THROUGH KNOWLEDGE SHARED"

CARVED OUT OF THE ENDURANCE OF GRANITE

GOD CREATED HIS MASTERPIECE—

THE CONFEDERATE SOLDIER

(This is a quote from Lillian Henderson,
author of Roster of Confederate Soldiers of Georgia, 1861–1865*)*

THIS MEMORIAL WALL IS DEDICATED TO

THE CONFEDERATE SOLDIERS WHOSE

HALLOWED REMAINS SLUMBER HERE BEFORE

IT. THEY WILL EVER BE REMEMBERED, AS

BRAVE AND HEROIC AS ANY IN ALL THE

ANNALS OF HISTORY. FOREVER KNOWN

NOW BY THEIR NAMES ETCHED HEREON.

DEDICATED APRIL 24, 1999

On the opposite side a Latin cross is carved on the center panel. Beneath the cross:

LEST WE FORGET

This monument is one of three quoting the words of Lillian Henderson. The others are in Atkinson County and Peach County.

The side panels contain pictures of local buildings and other sites significant in the war—the Blunt House, the Western and Atlantic Depot in Dalton, the Huff House, the Hamilton House, the Clisby Austin House, the railroad tunnel at Tunnel Hill, and Praters Mill.

On the center panel are carved the Great Seal of the Confederacy and the logos of the SCV and the UDC. The local SCV camp and UDC chapter are named.

The wall lists the Confederate soldiers buried in the cemetery. There are approximately 450 names. (A nearby Georgia Historic Commission marker, erected in 1956, states that the cemetery contains 421 unknown Confederates, 4 known Confederates, and 4 unknown Union dead.)

Wilcox County, Abbeville

LOCATION: North Broad Street, across from the courthouse	**DATE:** 1909
STYLE: Statue of a soldier on a column	**BUILDER:** UDC
FABRICATOR: McNeel Marble Co. (McNeel Memorials)	

CONFEDERATE DEAD

ERECTED BY THE
ABBEVILLE CHAPTER,
UNITED DAUGHTERS OF
THE CONFEDERACY,
APRIL 26, 1909.
IN MEMORY OF OUR
HEROES IN GRAY.

"THIS CARVEN STONE IS
HERE TO TELL
TO ALL THE WORLD THE
LOVE WE BEAR

TO THOSE WHO FOUGHT AND
BLED AND FELL,
WHOSE BATTLE CRY WAS
DO AND DARE.
WHO FEARED NO FOE, BUT
FACED THE FRAY—
OUR GALLANT MEN WHO
WORE THE GRAY."

"IT IS A DUTY WE OWE
TO POSTERITY TO SEE
THAT OUR CHILDREN SHALL
KNOW THE VIRTUES AND
BECOME WORTHY OF THEIR
SIRES."

*(Jefferson Davis, from 1882 speech
in New Orleans, with slight alteration
[Sedore, p. 91])*

The "carven stone" quote is inscribed on two monuments—this one and one in Fayetteville, Tennessee—but its source has not been found. (The words are referenced in Davis, p. 7.)

On the front of the plinth are crossed sabers, with "1861" above and "1865" below. "CONFEDERATE" is repeated on all four sides on the top step of the base.

The cost of the monument was $1,250. It originally had marble cannonballs on the corners (McKenney).

GEORGIA'S CONFEDERATE MONUMENTS

Wilcox County, Abbeville

LOCATION: Courthouse grounds, North Broad Street	**DATE:** 1925
STYLE: Memorial stone	**BUILDER:** Abbeville Daughters of the Confederacy

ERECTED JUNE 3, 1925
BY ABBEVILLE DAUGHTERS
OF THE CONFEDERACY
TO DEDICATE THE SPOT WHERE
JEFFERSON DAVIS
OUR GREAT CONFEDERATE LEADER
CAMPED MAY THE 9TH 1865
THE NIGHT BEFORE HIS CAPTURE.

LOVE MAKES MEMORY ETERNAL.

"LEST WE FORGET."

Wilkes County, Washington

LOCATION: Park in front of the courthouse, facing Robert Tombs Avenue		DATE: 1908
STYLE: Statue of a soldier on a column	BUILDERS: UDC, LMA, and Sons of Veterans	
FABRICATOR: McNeel Marble Co. (McNeel Memorials)		

ERECTED
ANNO DOMINI 1908
BY THE
"LAST CABINET" CHAPTER
UNITED
DAUGHTERS OF THE CONFEDERACY,
LADIES
MEMORIAL ASSOCIATION,
AND
SONS OF VETERANS.

A TRIBUTE
OF ABIDING LOVE
FOR OUR
CONFEDERATE HEROES.

CSA

1861–1865

MEN OF WILKES!
KNOW THROUGH ALL TIMES THAT
THEY
FOUGHT TO MAINTAIN A JUST UNION;
TO DEFEND CONSTITUTIONAL
GOVERNMENT;
TO PERPETUATE AMERICAN
LIBERTIES,
AND LEFT YOU THEIR PATRIOTIC
SPIRIT.
"LORD GOD OF HOSTS BE WITH US
YET,
LEST WE FORGET, LEST WE FORGET."

(From "Recessional" by Rudyard Kipling)

"ON FAME'S ETERNAL CAMPING
GROUND
THEIR SILENT TENTS ARE SPREAD,
AND GLORY GUARDS WITH SOLEMN
ROUND,
THE BIVOUAC OF THE DEAD."

*(From "The Bivouac of the Dead"
by Theodore O'Hara)*

The cost of the monument was $2,500 (McKenney). The front and rear of the column are decorated with a torn battle flag on a broken staff. A band of stars surrounds the column just below the statue. The soldier is standing at rest.

ON THIS SITE STOOD THE OLD GEORGIA STATE BANK BUILDING
IN WHICH PRES. DAVIS HELD THE LAST OFFICIAL MEETING OF THE
CONFEDERACY MAY 4, 1865

PRESENT

PRESIDENT JEFFERSON DAVIS
POSTM.GEN. JOHN H. REAGAN
SEC.OF NAVY STEPHEN R. MALLORY
SEC.OF WAR JOHN C. BRECKENRIDGE
ACT.SEC.OF TREAS. M. H. CLARK

ADJ.GEN. SAMUEL COOPER
NAV.PURCH.AGT. C. E. THOR BURN
MIL.ADV. GEN. BRAXTON BRAGG
COM.GEN. I. M. ST. JOHN

QM.GEN. A. R. LAWTON
PRVT.SEC. BURTON N. HARRISON
AIDE-DE-CAMP COL. J. T. WOOD
AIDE-DE-CAMP COL. LUBBOCK EX.GOV.TEX
AIDE-DE-CAMP COL. WM. P. JOHNSTON

AT THIS MEETING THE CONFEDERATE GOVERNMENT WAS DISSOLVED, THE LAST
OFFICIAL PAPERS WERE SIGNED, THE RESIDUE OF COIN AND BULLION BROUGHT
FROM RICHMOND WAS DISPOSED OF BY ORDER OF PRES. DAVIS, AND BOTH CIVIL
AND MILITARY OFFICIALS SEPARATED TO MAKE THEIR ESCAPE.

ERECTED BY LAST CABINET CHAPTER
UNITED DAUGHTERS OF THE CONFEDERACY
WASHINGTON, GEORGIA
1938

Wilkes County, Washington

LOCATION: Courthouse grounds, facing Court Street	DATE: 1938
STYLE: Memorial stone	BUILDER: UDC

ON THIS SITE STOOD THE OLD GEORGIA STATE BANK BUILDING
IN WHICH PRES. DAVIS HELD THE LAST OFFICIAL MEETING OF THE
CONFEDERACY MAY 4, 1865

AT THIS MEETING THE CONFEDERATE GOVERNMENT WAS
DISSOLVED, THE LAST
OFFICIAL PAPERS WERE SIGNED, THE RESIDUE OF COIN AND
BULLION BROUGHT
FROM RICHMOND WAS DISPOSED OF BY ORDER OF PRES. DAVIS,
AND BOTH CIVIL
AND MILITARY OFFICIALS SEPARATED TO MAKE THEIR ESCAPE.

ERECTED BY LAST CABINET CHAPTER
UNITED DAUGHTERS OF THE CONFEDERACY
WASHINGTON, GEORGIA—1938

At the top of the stone crossed battle flags are carved above the Great Seal of the Confederacy.

Those present at the meeting are listed. They include: President Jefferson Davis, Postmaster General John H. Reagan, Secretary of the Navy Stephen R. Mallory, Secretary of War John C. Breckinridge, Acting Secretary of the Treasury M. H. Clark, Adjutant General Samuel Cooper, Military Advisor General Braxton Bragg, and seven others.

Worth County, Sylvester

LOCATION: Courthouse grounds, facing North Main Street | **DATE:** 1989 | **STYLE:** Obelisk

IN HONOR AND MEMORY
OF THOSE FROM
WORTH COUNTY
WHO SACRIFICED
THEIR LIVES, THOSE
MISSING IN ACTION
AND THOSE WHO SERVED
IN THE DEFENSE
OF THEIR COUNTRY

AMERICAN
REVOLUTION
1775–1783

WAR BETWEEN
THE STATES
1861–1865

WAR OF 1812
1812–1815

SPANISH
AMERICAN WAR
1898

WORLD WAR I
1917–1918

WORLD WAR II
1941–1945

KOREA
1950–1953

VIETNAM
1964–1975

DEDICATED MAY 27, 1989

IN MEMORY OF THOSE WHO
DIED FROM WORTH COUNTY

Around the base are the words "LIBERTY," "COUNTRY," "JUSTICE," and "COURAGE."

On the sides of the obelisk, at the top, are the Great Seal of the United States and emblems of the different branches of service.

A bronze tablet at the entrance of the courthouse names the men of Worth County killed in the War Between the States, World War I, World War II, Korea, and Vietnam. The list includes 142 names from the War Between the States, more than twice the number of the other four combined.

IN HONOR AND MEMORY
OF THOSE FROM
WORTH COUNTY
WHO SACRIFICED
THEIR LIVES, THOSE
MISSING IN ACTION,
AND THOSE WHO SERVED
IN THE DEFENSE
OF THEIR COUNTRY

AMERICAN
REVOLUTION
1775 — 1783

WAR BETWEEN
THE STATES
1861 — 1865

LIBERTY

DEDICATED MAY 27, 1989

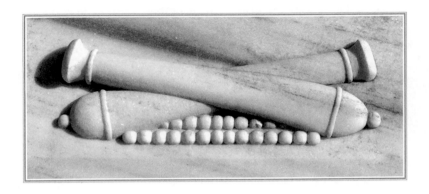

CITY AND COUNTY LISTINGS

CITY	COUNTY	CITY	COUNTY
Abbeville	Wilcox	Cordele	Crisp
Albany	Dougherty	Covington	Newton
Americus	Sumter	Crawfordville	Taliaferro
Andersonville	Sumter	Cumming	Forsyth
Appling	Columbia	Cusseta	Chattahoochee
Ashburn	Turner	Cuthbert	Randolph
Athens	Clarke		
Atlanta	Fulton	Dallas	Paulding
Augusta	Richmond	Dalton	Whitfield
		Darien	McIntosh
Bainbridge	Decatur	Dawson	Terrell
Baldwin	Banks	Dawsonville	Dawson
Barnesville	Lamar	Decatur	DeKalb
Baxley	Appling	Douglas	Coffee
Blairsville	Union	Douglasville	Douglas
Blakely	Early	Dublin	Laurens
Brunswick	Glynn		
Buena Vista	Marion	Eastman	Dodge
Butler	Taylor	Eatonton	Putnam
		Elberton	Elbert
Cairo	Grady	Ellaville	Schley
Calhoun	Gordon	Ellijay	Gilmer
Campbellton	Fulton	Evans	Columbia
Canton	Cherokee		
Carnesville	Franklin	Fairburn	Fulton
Carrollton	Carroll	Fayetteville	Fayette
Cartersville	Bartow	Forsyth	Monroe
Cassville	Bartow	Franklin	Heard
Cedartown	Polk	Fort Gaines	Clay
Chickamauga	Walker	Fort Gordon	Richmond
Clayton	Rabun		
Cochran	Bleckley	Gainesville	Hall
Colbert	Madison	Gray	Jones
Colquitt	Miller	Greensboro	Greene
Columbus	Muscogee	Griffin	Spalding
Commerce	Jackson	Grovetown	Columbia
Conyers	Rockdale	Guyton	Effingham

CITY	COUNTY	CITY	COUNTY
Hamilton	Harris	Newnan	Coweta
Hartwell	Hart		
Hawkinsville	Pulaski	Oakwood	Hall
Hazlehurst	Jeff Davis	Ocilla	Irwin
Hinesville	Liberty	Oglethorpe	Macon
		Oxford	Newton
Irwinville	Irwin		
		Palmetto	Fulton
Jackson	Butts	Pearson	Atkinson
Jefferson	Jackson	Pelham	Mitchell
Jeffersonville	Twiggs	Perry	Houston
Jonesboro	Clayton	Powersville	Peach
Kennesaw	Cobb	Quitman	Brooks
Kingston	Bartow		
		Resaca	Gordon
LaFayette	Walker	Richmond Hill	Bryan
LaGrange	Troup	Ringgold	Catoosa
Lawrenceville	Gwinnett	Roberta	Crawford
Lexington	Oglethorpe	Rome	Floyd
Lincolnton	Lincoln	Roswell	Fulton
Lovejoy	Clayton		
Lumpkin	Stewart	Sandersville	Washington
		Savannah	Chatham
Macon	Bibb	Sparta	Hancock
Madison	Morgan	Springfield	Effingham
Marietta	Cobb	Statesboro	Bulloch
McDonough	Henry	Stone Mountain	DeKalb
Menlo	Chattooga	Swainsboro	Emanuel
Milledgeville	Baldwin	Sylvania	Screven
Millen	Jenkins	Sylvester	Worth
Monroe	Walton		
Montezuma	Macon	Talbotton	Talbot
Monticello	Jasper	Tennille	Washington
Moultrie	Colquitt	Thomaston	Upson
Mount Vernon	Montgomery	Thomasville	Thomas
		Thomson	McDuffie

CITY	COUNTY	COUNTY	CITY
Tifton	Tift	Appling	Baxley
Toccoa	Stephens	Atkinson	Pearson
Trenton	Dade		
		Baldwin	Milledgeville
Union Point	Greene	Banks	Baldwin
		Bartow	Cartersville
Valdosta	Lowndes		Cassville
Vidalia	Toombs		Kingston
Vienna	Dooly	Bibb	Macon
		Bleckley	Cochran
Warrenton	Warren	Brantley	Waynesville
Washington	Wilkes	Brooks	Quitman
Watkinsville	Oconee	Bryan	Richmond Hill
Waycross	Ware	Bulloch	Statesboro
Waynesboro	Burke	Burke	Waynesboro
Waynesville	Brantley	Butts	Jackson
West Point	Troup		
Wrightsville	Johnson	Campbell	See Fulton
		Carroll	Carrollton
		Catoosa	Ringgold
		Chatham	Savannah
		Chattahoochee	Cusseta
		Chattooga	Menlo
		Cherokee	Canton
		Clarke	Athens
		Clay	Fort Gaines
		Clayton	Jonesboro
			Lovejoy
		Cobb	Kennesaw
			Marietta
		Coffee	Douglas
		Colquitt	Moultrie
		Columbia	Appling
			Evans
			Grovetown
		Coweta	Newnan
		Crawford	Roberta

COUNTY	CITY	COUNTY	CITY
Crisp	Cordele	Hall	Gainesville
			Oakwood
Dade	Trenton	Hancock	Sparta
Dawson	Dawsonville	Harris	Hamilton
Decatur	Bainbridge	Hart	Hartwell
DeKalb	Decatur	Heard	Franklin
	Stone Mountain	Henry	McDonough
Dodge	Eastman	Houston	Perry
Dooly	Vienna		
Dougherty	Albany	Irwin	Irwinville
Douglas	Douglasville		Ocilla
Early	Blakely	Jackson	Commerce
Effingham	Guyton		Jefferson
	Springfield	Jasper	Monticello
Elbert	Elberton	Jeff Davis	Hazlehurst
Emanuel	Swainsboro	Jenkins	Millen
		Johnson	Wrightsville
Fayette	Fayetteville	Jones	Gray
Floyd	Rome		
Forsyth	Cumming	Lamar	Barnesville
Franklin	Carnesville	Laurens	Dublin
Fulton	Atlanta	Lee	See Dougherty
	Campbellton	Liberty	Hinesville
	Fairburn	Lincoln	Lincolnton
	Palmetto	Lowndes	Valdosta
	Roswell		
		Macon	Montezuma
			Oglethorpe
Gilmer	Ellijay	Madison	Colbert
Glynn	Brunswick	Marion	Buena Vista
Gordon	Calhoun	McDuffie	Thomson
	Resaca	McIntosh	Darien
Grady	Cairo	Miller	Colquitt
Greene	Greensboro	Mitchell	Pelham
	Union Point	Monroe	Forsyth
Gwinnett	Lawrenceville	Montgomery	Mount Vernon

COUNTY	CITY	COUNTY	CITY
Morgan	Madison		West Point
Muscogee	Columbus	Turner	Ashburn
		Twiggs	Jeffersonville
Newton	Covington		
	Oxford	Union	Blairsville
		Upson	Thomaston
Oconee	Watkinsville		
Oglethorpe	Lexington	Walker	Chickamauga
			LaFayette
Paulding	Dallas	Walton	Monroe
Peach	Powersville	Ware	Waycross
Polk	Cedartown	Warren	Warrenton
Pulaski	Hawkinsville	Washington	Sandersville
Putnam	Eatonton		Tennille
		Whitfield	Dalton
Rabun	Clayton	Wilcox	Abbeville
Randolph	Cuthbert	Wilkes	Washington
Richmond	Augusta	Worth	Sylvester
	Fort Gordon		
Rockdale	Conyers		
Schley	Ellaville		
Screven	Sylvania		
Spalding	Griffin		
Stephens	Toccoa		
Stewart	Lumpkin		
Sumter	Americus		
	Andersonville		
Talbot	Talbotton		
Taliaferro	Crawfordville		
Taylor	Butler		
Terrell	Dawson		
Thomas	Thomasville		
Tift	Tifton		
Toombs	Vidalia		
Troup	LaGrange		

BIBLIOGRAPHY

Bragg, William Harris. *Joe Brown's Army: The Georgia State Line 1862-1865*. Macon GA: Mercer University Press, 1987.

Buzzett, Isabell Smith. *Confederate Monuments of Georgia*. Atlanta Chapter 18, United Daughters of the Confederacy, 1984.

Castel, Albert. *Decision in the West*. Lawrence: University Press of Kansas, 1992.

Confederate Veteran 24/7 (July 1916).

Confederate Veteran 29/8 (August 1921).

Confederated Southern Memorial Association. *History of the Confederated Memorial Associations of the South*. New Orleans: Graham Press, 1904. Cited as CSMA.

Davis, Stephen. "Empty Eyes, Marble Hand: The Confederate Monument and the South," *Journal of Popular Culture* 16/3 (Winter 1982): 2–21.

Evans, Clement A., editor. *Confederate Military History*. Atlanta: Confederate Publishing Co., 1899.

Jones, Jr., Charles C. *Address Delivered before the Confederate Survivors' Association in Augusta, Georgia, on Memorial Day, April 26, 1893*. Augusta GA: Chronicle Job Printing Company, 1893.

Knight, Lucian Lamar. *Georgia's Landmarks, Memorials, and Legends*. 1913; reprinted, Gretna LA: Pelican Publishing Company, Inc., 2006.

Marshall, Charlotte Thomas. *Oconee Hill Cemetery of Athens, Georgia*. Athens GA: Athens Historical Society, 2009.

McKenney, Frank M. *The Standing Army*. Alpharetta GA: W. H. Wolfe and Associates, 1993.

McNeel Marble Co., *McNeel Memorials*. 1921, reprinted, Marietta GA: G. Warren Thomas, 2008. Cited as McNeel Memorials. This booklet lists numerous Georgia monuments built as of the date of publication. An original is located in the Georgia Room of the Cobb County Library in Marietta. According to Thomas, the copy in the Cobb library is the only original known to exist.

Rodgers, Robert L. *History—Confederate Veterans' Association of Fulton County, Georgia*. Atlanta: V. P. Sisson, Publisher, 1890.

Sedore, Timothy S. *An Illustrated Guide to Virginia's Confederate Monuments*. Carbondale IL: Southern Illinois University Press, 2011.

Snowden, Yates, editor. *History of South Carolina*. Chicago and New York: Lewis Publishing Company, 1920.

Helen P. Trimpi, *Crimson Confederate: Harvard Men Who Fought for the South*. Knoxville: University of Tennessee Press, 2010.

Underwood, J. L. *The Women of the Confederacy*. New York and Washington: Neale Publishing Co., 1906.

United Daughters of the Confederacy, Georgia Division. *Confederate Monuments and Markers in Georgia*. Fernandina Beach FL: Wolfe Publishing, 2002. Cited as UDC 2002.

Widener, Ralph W., Jr. *Confederate Monuments: Enduring Symbols of the South and the War between the States*. Washington: Andromeda Associates, 1982.

Wiggins, David N. *Georgia's Confederate Monuments and Cemeteries*. Charleston SC: Arcadia Publications, 2006.

William Collins, "An Ode Written at the Beginning of the Year 1746"

Paul Hayne, "The Will and the Wing"

Sidney Alroy Jonas, "Lines on a Confederate Note"

Sidney Lanier, "The Marshes of Glynn"

R. W. Lillard, "America's Answer"

Theodore O'Hara, "The Bivouac of the Dead"

James R. Randall, "Maryland, My Maryland"

Pearl Rivers, "The Soldier's Grave"

Abram J. Ryan: "The Conquered Banner," "C.S.A.," "The Sword of Robert Lee," "A Land Without Ruins," "Sentinel Songs," "Epitaph," "The March of the Deathless Dead"

Francis O. Ticknor, "Under the Willows"

Henry Van Dyke, "God of the Open Air"

James Greenleaf Whittier, "The Female Martyr"

Philip Stanhope Worsley, "The Grand Old Bard Who Never Dies"

    Many monuments quote the famous lines written by Philip Stanhope Worsley, an English poet whose translation of *The Iliad* was published in 1865: "No nation rose so white and fair, / None fell so pure of crime."

    Worsley presented a copy of his translation of the epic to Robert E. Lee, which Lee received in February 1866. The copy presented to Lee contained a poem, written in Worsley's own hand, the first lines of which were "The grand old bard who never dies." The text cites this source as "The Grand Old Bard."

ON-LINE SOURCES AND BROCHURES

    The text cites several online sources. The author has retained printed copies of the pages containing the information referenced. In a few cases, the sources are brochures printed for dedication ceremonies or other purposes. The author has retained copies of these as well.